A LENTEN JOURNEY
WITH THE SAINTS

Abide with Us

The Foundry Publishing®
PO Box 419527
Kansas City, MO 64141
thefoundrypublishing.com

ISBN 978-0-8341-4226-8

Printed in the
United States of America

Cover design: Caines Design
Interior design: Caines Design/Sharon Page

Readings compiled from Al Truesdale, ed., *The Book of Saints*, 5 vols. (Kansas City:
Beacon Hill Press of Kansas City, 2013-18).

Note: To improve readability, it has been necessary to paraphrase many of the pub-
lic-domain compositions featured in this book.

The internet addresses, email addresses, and phone numbers in this book are accurate
at the time of publication. They are provided as a resource. The Foundry Publishing®
does not endorse them or vouch for their content or permanence.

10 9 8 7 6 5 4 3 2 1

# About the Author

Al Truesdale, PhD, a native South Carolinian, is emeritus professor of philosophy of religion and Christian ethics at Nazarene Theological Seminary. He is a graduate of Trevecca Nazarene University, Nazarene Theological Seminary, and Emory University, where he earned a PhD in Systematic Theology. Dr. Truesdale is the editor of numerous books, including the *Global Wesleyan Dictionary of Theology*, *The Book of Saints* (5 vols.), *God Reconsidered: The Promise and Peril of Process Theology*, and, more recently, *The Pastor as Theological Steward*. He is also the author of *If God Is God, Then Why?*, *Confessing Christ as Lord of All in a Pluralistic World*, and the forthcoming *Lord of the Tragic* (The Foundry Publishing). He is an ordained elder in the Church of the Nazarene and has served as pastor of congregations in North Carolina, Georgia, and Massachusetts. He also served Eastern Nazarene College as professor of religion and more recently as interim president. He and his wife, Esther, live in the coastal plain region of South Carolina. They have three daughters, three grandchildren, and one great-grandchild.

# Contents

# Introduction

Writing from a Roman prison, the apostle Paul addressed the church at Philippi in commendable language. Unlike some of his other epistles, not one word of criticism appears, only words of approval, hope, confidence, and encouragement. Yet he recognizes their Christian journey is incomplete. The Lord who began a good work in them will one day bring it to completion (Phil. 1:6).

At the heart of Paul's theology resides a careful balance between the "already" and the "not yet." Already the "fruits of righteousness which come through Jesus Christ, to the glory and praise of God," are being produced in the Philippians (1:11). But using himself as an example, Paul says Christians have not yet been made perfect (3:12). Nevertheless, Paul is pressing on "toward the goal for the prize of the upward call of God in Christ Jesus" (v. 14).

The season of Lent, the six weeks from Ash Wednesday to Easter, is positioned between the already and the not yet. It has nothing to do with being bound to the old life of captivity to sin, spiritual defeat, and paralysis. And it certainly has nothing to do with superficially giving up some things. That would be pagan, not Christian. With Gregory the Great (540–604), Christians confidently pray, "Oft in fast and prayer with thee, our spirits strengthen with thy grace, and give us joy to see thy face."[1]

Confession that marks the season of Lent and preparation for Easter occurs in a spirit of openness and honesty and sober reflection upon and an inventory of our need of a redeemer. All of this is bathed in hope and confidence that the promised day of the Lord will mark the consummation of God's kingdom in us and in God's creation. Easter guarantees this.

For Christians, Lent unfolds in an environment of ongoing sanctification of the whole of life (cf. Rom. 1:7; Gk., "appointed to holiness"). It is marked by confident yearning and anticipation, often including fasting. But make no mistake, it is characterized by confession and forgiveness. It is confession for the ways and times we and our Christian sisters and brothers have not borne the "fruits of righteousness" and have not faithfully identified with our suffering Lord. It is also confession for the inadequacy of our testimony to a broken world. The apostle Paul's admission that he had not yet been made perfect was made in full confidence that God's grace enfolds an honest admission of the "not yet," an honesty that rests upon confidence that what Christ has begun he will complete.

From diverse perspectives and periods in church history, the voices of the "saints" that follow bear witness to the Spirit-aided Christian journey from the "already" to the "not yet."

> *Through these days of penitence,*
> *And through your Passion-tide,*
> *Forevermore, in life and death,*
> *O Lord, with us abide.*
>
> *Abide with us that when this life*
> *Of suffering is past,*
> *An Easter of unending joy*
> *We may attain at last![2]*

## DAY 1

# Ash Wednesday

## READING FOR THE DAY

We are commanded in Scripture to "put off" the old sinful self and to "put on the new self, created to be like God in true righteousness and holiness." Now it must be admitted that this is a very difficult challenge. But it is not impossible. Many happy souls have been assisted by divine power to bring it to pass. Then why should we despair of success? Is God's hand shortened that it cannot save? Was he the God of our fathers only? Is he not the God of their children also? Yes, doubtless, of their children also.

This is a task that will cause us some pain, for it will require us to part with some cherished aspirations, maybe to part with a friend, to crucify some cherished passion that might be exceedingly dear to us, perhaps as difficult to abandon as to cut off a hand or pluck out an eye. But so what? Will we not be made a real living member of Christ, a child of God, and an inheritor of the kingdom of heaven? Undoubtedly we will be.

George Whitefield (1714-70), "On Regeneration,"
*Selected Sermons*, sermon 49

## PRAYER

O LORD MY GOD, perfect us in such patience that we may be in no haste to escape from toil or loneliness or suffering; yet ever in haste to serve you, to please you, and, when you will, to go home to your blessed presence. Amen.

Christina Georgina Rossetti (1830-94), *Prayers: Ancient and Modern*, p. 363

## FOR REFLECTION

Ps. 119:33-40; Isa. 59:1; Jer. 29:11-14; Matt. 5:29; 6:25-34; Luke 6:46-49; Rom. 6:1-14; Gal. 5:16-26; 6:7-10; Eph. 3:14-21; 4:24; Col. 1:9-14

## QUESTIONS FOR CONSIDERATION

1. George Whitefield calls Christians to a sober soul-searching in order to reveal things in their lives not yet purged by the Holy Spirit. How is such soul-searching and cleansing related to God's grace and to Christian holiness?

_____

_____

_____

_____

_____

_____

_____

_____

_____

_____

_____

2. Lent is a time for the personal "putting off" of things contrary to God's will, and it is a task for the whole body of Christ. What aspects of the church's witness in the world need to be more closely aligned with its Lord?

_____

_____

_____

_____

_____

_____

_____

_____

3. In her prayer, Christina Rossetti asks for patience. In what areas of your life should this discipline be increased?

_____

_____

_____

_____

_____

_____

_____

_____

_____

_____

# Thursday

## FEBRUARY 15, 2024

## READING FOR THE DAY

If God's essence is that he is holy, it is equally essential that he judge what is unholy. Human dignity is better assured if we are broken in judgment by God's holiness than if God were to ignore his own holiness and leave us as we are. God's holy order is as essential to humankind's well-being as it is to God's. That is why the holy satisfaction Christ made to God's holiness on the cross provides a new—restored and reconciled—humanity. Any form of Christianity that omits God's judging holiness against sin contributes to human degradation. From a reduced divine holiness, no salvation comes, nor could human dignity survive.

We must have a gospel that decides the eternal destiny of humankind. Unless the holiness of God were practically and adequately established, there could be no real, deep, permanent change in the sinner or in this alienated world.

That is what Christ accomplished on the cross. The judgment-death of Christ set up a real and actual kingdom of holiness, a truth easier for faith to see than for theology to explain.

Peter T. Forsyth (1848–1921), *The Work of Christ*, chap. 4

## PRAYER

FATHER IN HEAVEN, you alone are holy, your way, O God, is holy, and Holy is your name: Grant unto us sinners a godly fear of your righteous judgment and also hearts of utter thanksgiving that you clothe us in the righteousness of your Son that we should be holy and blameless before you, through the same Jesus Christ, who with the Holy Spirit reigns, one God, now and forever. Amen.

The Very Reverend Frank F. Limehouse III

## FOR REFLECTION

Ps. 36:6; Isa. 5:16; 6:1–5; 47:4; 57:15; Matt. 7:21–23; Acts 10:34–43; 2 Cor. 7:1; Eph. 1:4; 2 Tim. 4:1–5; 1 Pet. 1:14–16; 2 Pet. 1:2–8

## QUESTIONS FOR CONSIDERATION

1. We often speak of God's love for us. How is God's judgment an expression of his love?

_____

_____

_____

_____

_____

_____

2. God's holiness refers to God being God alone. He alone is to be worshipped. In this season of Lent, in what areas of your life does your worship of God alone need to be improved?

_____

_____

_____

_____

_____

_____

_____

3. God's holiness assures Christians safety against all threats from supposed "gods." What areas of your life need to be more fully entrusted to God's holy care?

_____

_____

_____

_____

_____

_____

4. Do the commandments of God gain their authority because they have value independent of God, or do they have authority because they express the character and will of God?

_____

_____

_____

_____

_____

_____

# DAY 3
## Friday
### FEBRUARY 16, 2024

## READING FOR THE DAY

The cross is laid on every Christian. The first Christ-suffering which every man must experience is the call to abandon the attachments of this world. It is that dying of the old man which is the result of his encounter with Christ. As we embark upon discipleship we surrender ourselves to Christ in union with his death—we give over our lives to death. Thus it begins: the cross is not the terrible end to an otherwise god-fearing and happy life, but it meets us at the beginning of our communion with Christ. When Christ calls a man, he bids him come and die. It may be a death like that of the first disciples who had to leave home and work to follow [Jesus]. . . . But it is the same death every time—death in Jesus Christ, the death of the old man at [Jesus's] call.

Dietrich Bonhoeffer (1906-45), *The Cost of Discipleship*, chap. 4

## PRAYER

OUR FATHER IN HEAVEN, whose Son taught us that "whoever would save his life will lose it, and whoever loses his life for [your] sake will find it": Bring death, we pray, to the old Adam in us, and grant us with born-again hearts to say in truth and sincerity, "I have been crucified with Christ; it is no longer I who live, but Christ who lives in me; and the life

I now live in the flesh I live by faith in the Son of God, who loved me and gave himself for me." Amen.

The Very Reverend Frank F. Limehouse III; Matt. 16:25; Gal. 2:20

## FOR REFLECTION

Matt. 5:1–12; 9:17; 10:38; 16:25; John 3:3; Rom. 6:1–6; Gal. 2:20; 5:16–18; Eph. 4:22–24; Phil. 3:7–11; 4:8–9; Col. 3:9–17; Titus 2:12–13; Heb. 12:3; 1 Pet. 1:14

## QUESTIONS FOR CONSIDERATION

1. Lent is a discreet time for asking again if we have "died" as Bonhoeffer describes. Are there dimensions of your life that have yet to be crucified by Christ?

\
\
\
\
\
\
\
\

2. The apostle Paul tells us that crucifixion of the old self must precede the resurrection of a new Christ-centered person (Rom. 6:1–5). Have you permitted the Holy Spirit to inventory your "crucifixion"?

\
\
\

_____

_____

_____

_____

_____

_____

3. If Christians have once been crucified with Christ, why must careful self-examination by the Holy Spirit continue? Why must Christians die "daily"?

_____

_____

_____

_____

_____

_____

_____

_____

_____

DAY 4

# Saturday

## FEBRUARY 17, 2024

(When in 1937 Mother Teresa was about to make her profession of perpetual vows, she wrote a letter to her former confessor, Jesuit Father Franjo Jambrekoviç, in which she expressed the secret of God's work in her life.)

## READING FOR THE DAY

I really cannot thank God enough for all that He has done for me. His for all eternity! Now I rejoice with my whole heart that I have joyfully carried my cross with Jesus. There were sufferings—there were moments when my eyes were filled with tears—but thanks be to God for everything. . . .

Do not think that my spiritual life is strewn with roses—that is the flower which I hardly ever find on my way. Quite the contrary, I have more often as my companion "darkness."[3] And when the night becomes very thick—and it seems to me as if I will end up in hell—then I simply offer myself to Jesus. If He wants me to go there—I am ready—but only under the condition that it really makes Him happy. I need much grace, much of Christ's strength to persevere in trust, in that blind love which leads only to Jesus Crucified.

Mother Teresa (1910-97), *Mother Teresa: Come Be My Light*, p. 20

## PRAYER

MERCIFUL FATHER, who gives strength to the weak, when we are overcome with the crosses we must carry, give us the hope we need to say from our hearts: "We are afflicted in every way, but not crushed; . . . always carrying in the body the death of Jesus, so that the life of Jesus may also be manifested in our bodies." Amen.

The Very Reverend Frank F. Limehouse III; 2 Cor. 4:8, 10

## FOR REFLECTION

1 Kings 19:1-18; Ps. 42:1-11; Matt. 11:29; 26:36-46; Mark 8:34-35; 14:35-36; John 15:1-7; 1 Cor. 10:13; 2 Cor. 4:8-10; Phil. 2:5-8; Heb. 12:3-24; 1 Pet. 5:6-10

## QUESTIONS FOR CONSIDERATION

1. Though a model of Christian holiness and service, Mother Teresa admits to times of "darkness" in her life. Is "darkness" compatible with "holiness" as Mother Teresa indicates? How can this contrast be explained?

_____

_____

_____

_____

_____

_____

_____

_____

2. The "darkness" to which Mother Teresa refers calls to mind The "darkness" Jesus suffered in the garden of Gethsemane and on the cross. Jesus called his disciples to "take up their cross and follow [him]" (Matt. 10:38, NIV). In your world—social, domestic, economic—what might it mean to suffer with the suffering Christ?

_____

_____

_____

_____

_____

_____

_____

3. We often speak of how Christ is manifest in healing. How might Christ be manifest in our suffering?

_____

_____

_____

_____

_____

_____

_____

_____

_____

# First Sunday in Lent

## FEBRUARY 18, 2024

## READING FOR THE DAY

Dear Sir,
Today I learned that most probably you are the one who betrayed me. I went through 10 months of concentration camp. My father died after 9 days of imprisonment. My sister died in prison. . . .

The harm you planned has turned into good for me by God. I came nearer to Him. A severe punishment is awaiting you. I have prayed for you, that the Lord may accept you if you will repent. Think that the Lord Jesus on the cross also took your sins upon Himself. If you accept this and want to be His child, you are saved for eternity.

I have forgiven you everything. God will also forgive you everything, if you ask Him. He loves you. He loves you and He Himself sent His Son to Earth to reconcile your sins, which meant to suffer the punishment for you and me. You, on your part, have to give an answer to this. If He says, "Come unto Me, give Me your heart," then your answer must be: "Yes, Lord, I come, make me your child."

Corrie ten Boom (1892–1983), *Prison Letters*, p. 81

## PRAYER

FATHER IN HEAVEN, who has taught us to forgive others as you have forgiven us, for by doing so we will draw nearer to you: Drive far from us the hatred that destroys our souls. Endue your children with the love we need to do as you command, that our witness might draw others to the repentance they need to stand blameless in the day of your righteous judgment, through the merits of Jesus Christ. Amen.

The Very Reverend Frank F. Limehouse III

## FOR REFLECTION

Gen. 33:1-14; 50:15-21; Pss. 103:10-14; 130:3; Matt. 6:12, 14-15; 18:21-22; Mark 11:25; Luke 6:27; 15:25-32; 17:3-4; Rom. 12:14-21; Eph. 4:32

## QUESTIONS FOR CONSIDERATION

1. Corrie ten Boom's act of forgiveness complied with her Lord's instructions to forgive as we have been forgiven (Matt. 6:9-13). In this season of Lent, are there unfinished acts of forgiveness you need to complete?

_____

_____

_____

_____

_____

_____

_____

2. Frank Limehouse prays, "Drive far from us the hatred that destroys our souls." How does a failure to forgive others wound our own souls?

_____

_____

_____

_____

_____

_____

_____

_____

3. Jesus was keenly aware of our readiness to accept forgiveness and of our reluctance to extend forgiveness to others (Matt. 18:21-35). What root problem underlies this reluctance? Why is a willingness to accept God's forgiveness, and God's grace, inseparable from a willingness to forgive others?

_____

_____

_____

_____

_____

_____

_____

_____

4. Reflect on the discord, the social and individual carnage, that a refusal to forgive has visited on humankind.

_____

_____

_____

_____

_____

_____

_____

_____

_____

_____

# DAY 5
## Monday
### FEBRUARY 19, 2024

## READING FOR THE DAY

The God of the Bible is the strangest thing about the whole Bible. In the history of religion, there is no other like the God of the Bible. . . . That is hard to understand. So the peoples who dealt with God in the Bible always wanted to relate to the Divine Self like they related to . . . other notions of God. And in every time, even ours, we are tempted to force God into . . . categories as though God belongs to a species of similar agents.

But God is not like any other. And God's strangeness is in this. God is *with people*. God is *for people*. God's goodness is not in the great transcendental power nor in the majestic remoteness nor in the demanding toughness but in the readiness to be with and for people. . . . This being with and for is not a matter of bribery or deception or intimidation. God simply wills it so.

Walter Brueggemann (1933– ), *The Bible Makes Sense*, p. 35

## PRAYER

BLESS THE LORD, O MY SOUL; and all that is in me praise his holy name. Bless the Lord, O my soul; and forget not all his benefits. O that I might worship you with every faculty of my soul, gracious God; that I might worthily thank you for every manifestation of your mercy; my God, my Strength, enlighten my mind and set ablaze the devotion of my heart; through Jesus Christ, who lives and reigns with you and the Holy Spirit, one God eternal. Amen.

Adapted from Augustine (AD 354–430), Bishop of Hippo, "Praise to God," in *Prayers from the Collection of the Late Baron Bunsen*, pp. 147-48

## FOR REFLECTION

Josh. 1:9; Pss. 23:1-6; 73:23-28; 103:1-2; 139:7-10; Isa. 40:9-14; 41:10; 43:1-3; 49:13; Matt. 1:18-25; 28:16-20; John 1:1-18; 10:11; 14:16-17, 25-29; Rom. 8:38-39

## QUESTIONS FOR CONSIDERATION

1. The season of Lent offers a prime opportunity to examine ways we might have acted as though God is just one more "god" among others. Ask the Holy Spirit to search you for places and ways idolatry might lurk in your life.

_____

_____

_____

_____

_____

_____

2. Walter Brueggemann speaks comfortingly of God being with us. First, reflect on the peace of God being with us and, second, on why God being with us must not descend into taking God's presence for granted and excluding worship and thanksgiving.

_____

_____

_____

_____

_____

_____

3. What tempting forms does idolatry assume in our culture?

_____

_____

_____

_____

_____

4. The Gospel of Matthew affirms that Jesus fulfills the prophecy in Isaiah 7:14 and is the child Isaiah calls Immanuel (or "God with us") (Matt. 2:23, NIV; see vv. 18–23). Does the incarnation mean that God ceases to be the transcendent Creator who sustains his creation moment by moment? Reflect on the mystery of the incarnation.

_____

_____

_____

_____

_____

_____

# Tuesday

## FEBRUARY 20, 2024

## READING FOR THE DAY

Unless the Spirit controls our lives, we will be dominated by our old sinful nature. . . .

. . . We must deal completely with sin in our lives if we are to know the infilling of the Holy Spirit. . . . Pride is often at the root of our sins, and our pride is often deeply wounded when we honestly admit before God and before men that we are not as good as we had thought we were.

Dealing with sin . . . is also hard . . . because we must not only know our sin, but we must repent of it. And some of us may be harboring sin . . . , unwilling to give it up. . . .

. . . We must not be content with a casual examination of our lives. . . . We must confess not only what we think is sin, but what the Holy Spirit labels as sin when we . . . listen to His voice from the Word of God. . . . Confession should be as broad as sin.

Billy Graham (1918–2018), *The Holy Spirit*, p. 138

## PRAYER

FATHER IN HEAVEN, whose Son taught us that the first
work of the Holy Spirit is to "convince the world concerning sin and righteousness and judgment": Because our sins
are ever before us, and also sins that are hidden from us in
the darkness of our own hearts, shine the divine light of the
Holy Spirit into our hearts that we might more clearly see our
wretchedness and earnestly repent by falling "beneath the
cross of Jesus," where "two wonders I confess—the wonders
of redeeming love and [our] unworthiness." Amen.

The Very Reverend Frank F. Limehouse III; Elizabeth C. Clephane,
"Beneath the Cross of Jesus" (1868); Hymnary; John 16:8

## FOR REFLECTION

Ps. 32:5; Prov. 28:13; John 16:12-15; Acts 19:11-20; Rom. 8:1-17;
2 Cor. 5:10; Gal. 5:13-24; Eph. 4:17–5:2; James 5:16; 1 Pet. 1:1-2;
2:4-12; 1 John 1:10; 2:1

## QUESTIONS FOR CONSIDERATION

1. Billy Graham clearly stated the ongoing need for the Holy
   Spirit to have free reign to search and cleanse us. Is such
   honesty a sign of faith and spiritual growth or a sign of
   defeat and immaturity?

_____

_____

_____

_____

_____

_____

_____

_____

2. How can such openness be a testimony to those who are
   not Christians?

_____

_____

_____

_____

_____

_____

_____

_____

_____

3. Frank Limehouse teaches us to pray, "Shine the divine
   light of the Holy Spirit into our hearts." Reflect on this
   invitation as an invitation both to self-examination and to
   Christian joy.

_____

_____

_____

_____

_____

_____

_____

_____

_____

DAY 7

# Wednesday

## FEBRUARY 21, 2024

## READING FOR THE DAY

The prayer of the heart . . . does not allow us to limit our relationship with God to interesting words or pious emotions. By its very nature such prayer transforms our whole being into Christ precisely because it opens the eyes of our soul to the truth of ourselves as well as to the truth of God. In our heart we come to see ourselves as sinners embraced by the mercy of God. It is this vision that makes us cry out, "Lord Jesus Christ, Son of the Living God, have mercy on me, a sinner." The prayer of the heart challenges us to hide absolutely nothing from God and to surrender ourselves unconditionally to his mercy.

Thus the prayer of the heart is the prayer of truth. It unmasks the many illusions about ourselves and about God and leads us into the true relationship of the sinner to the merciful God.

Henri Nouwen (1932-96), The Way of the Heart, pp. 78-79

## PRAYER

O MOST MERCIFUL FATHER, who has taught us that works without faith is dead, but also faith without works is dead: We frail sinners fall woefully short of your expectations for Christian discipleship, yet amazingly you take us back over and over again, like a child running into the lap of a mother's steadfast love. Increase our faith, we beseech you, that we might find the strength we need to walk the demanding journey of discipleship—not to earn your love, but to show our love and gratitude for your mercy and grace, through Jesus Christ our Lord and Savior. Amen.

*The Very Reverend Frank F. Limehouse III*

## FOR REFLECTION

Pss. 37:7; 96:5; 139:1; Jer. 16:17; 23:24; Matt. 16:24–26; Mark 14:36; John 17:17; Rom. 10:9–10; Eph. 1:13–14; Heb. 4:13; James 1:18; 2:14–26; 5:16; 2 Pet. 1:4; 1 John 1:9

## QUESTIONS FOR CONSIDERATION

1. Henri Nouwen has surely captured the meaning of Lent. If the gospel of Jesus Christ is good news, in what way is Lent good news about God, ourselves, and our world?

_____

_____

_____

_____

_____

_____

_____

2. Frank Limehouse prays for our faith to increase. Consider the relationship between the self-examination Lent requires and the increase of faith in our redeemer God.

_____

_____

_____

_____

_____

_____

3. Nouwen urges us to make the worship of God central to our prayers so that the "many illusions about ourselves and about God" may be revealed. What is the difference between worship and petition in prayer?

_____

_____

_____

_____

_____

4. Is prayer that excludes worship truly Christian?

_____

_____

_____

_____

_____

_____

# Thursday

## FEBRUARY 22, 2024

## READING FOR THE DAY

When the hour arrived for Jesus to ascend to his Father, his disciples were depressed. The thought of being separated from the one they loved, the bulwark against their weakness, and the center of their hopes, was bitter. Attentive to their sorrow, Jesus promised that upon returning to the Father he would send them a Comforter, the Holy Spirit, who would lead them into all truth. He would restore their sagging courage and abide with them to the end of the world. The promise was fulfilled in the mystery we commemorate today. On this day the Spirit of God, the Source of our sanctification, descended and enriched the disciples with his gifts. By his graces he formed them in the most perfect Christian virtues. The blessings of Pentecost were not confined to the apostles. They are perpetual for Jesus's disciples. The Spirit replenishes our hearts with gifts, adorns us with lovely ornaments, invigorates us by his power, and draws us to himself in ardent love. The effects of his coming must be proportionally the same as for the apostles. We should consider how the apostles conducted themselves after receiving the Holy Spirit and then compare their lives with our own.

Archbishop John Carroll, SJ (1735–1815), Sermon preached on Pentecost Sunday (n.d.), American Catholic Sermons, Carton 16

## PRAYER

HEAVENLY FATHER, you were faithful to send upon your disciples the promised Holy Spirit, the Comforter, in the flaming fire of holy love. Grant to your church fervency in the unity of the faith, that evermore abiding in you, your people may be made steadfast in Christian faith and active in the faith that works through love, through Jesus Christ our Lord. Amen.

"Whitsuntide," Prayers for Sacred Seasons,
*Ancient Collects and Other Prayers*, p. 63

## FOR REFLECTION

Luke 4:1-3; John 7:37-40; 14:15-27; 16:5-15; Acts 2:1-12; Rom. 8:1-17; 1 Cor. 2:1-16; 12:1-13; Gal. 5:16-26; Eph. 1:15-23; 6:10-18

## QUESTIONS FOR CONSIDERATION

1. In Christian discipleship, Lent and Pentecost cannot be separated. What is there about Lenten self-examination that anticipates and necessitates the Pentecostal gift of the Holy Spirit?

_____

_____

_____

_____

_____

_____

_____

_____

2. Archbishop John Carroll identifies the Holy Spirit as the "Source of our sanctification." Is this correct, or is Jesus Christ the source of our sanctification? If the latter, what is the role of the Holy Spirit? (Hint: consider "administrator" [John 15:26–27; 16:5–11].)

_____

_____

_____

_____

_____

_____

_____

_____

3. The New Testament speaks of the "gifts" (see 1 Cor. 12:4–11) and "fruit" (see Gal. 5:22–23) of the Holy Spirit. Are the gifts and fruit *provided* by the Holy Spirit, or are the gifts and fruit *secured* by Christ in his life, death, and resurrection? If the latter is true, what is the role of the Holy Spirit?

_____

_____

_____

_____

_____

_____

_____

_____

# DAY 9
## *Friday*
### FEBRUARY 23, 2024

## READING FOR THE DAY

It is the grand, essential, and practical characteristic of true Christians that, relying on God's promise to repenting sinners, they will be accepted through the Redeemer. They must renounce all masters other than Jesus Christ and unreservedly devote themselves to God. This is what baptism should daily teach us. We bring ourselves to the altar, consecrate ourselves to the proper Owner, and vow eternal hostility against the enemies of our salvation. Christians are sworn enemies of sin and hold no conference with it. There are no terms for peace.

As their reasonable service, Christians yield themselves to their rightful Sovereign without reserve, for they no longer belong to themselves. Their physical and mental faculties; their natural and acquired endowments; their substance, authority, time, and influence—all are but instruments to be employed in God's service. To this controlling principle all other principles are subordinate. What had been their ruling passion, their consuming pursuit, whether sensual or intellectual, of taste, fancy, or feeling, now occupies a secondary place or, more correctly, come under the rule of its true and legitimate superior.

William Wilberforce (1759–1833), *A Practical View of the Prevailing Religious System of Professed Christians*, chap. 1, sec. 1

## PRAYER

GRANT, LORD, we beseech you, to your people an inviolable firmness of faith, that as they confess your only begotten Son, the eternal Partaker of your glory, born in our very flesh of the Virgin Mother, they may be delivered from present adversities and admitted into the joys of your eternal kingdom, through Jesus Christ our Lord. Amen.

"Christmas," Prayers for Sacred Seasons, in
*Ancient Collects and Other Prayers,* p. 23

## FOR REFLECTION

Gen. 22:1–19; Exod. 3:1–4:17; Job 11:13–15; 31:5–8; Ps. 37:1–7; Jon. 2:1–10; Matt. 6:33–34; John 5:24–27; Rom. 6:1–4; 8:12–17; 12:1–2, 9–13

## QUESTIONS FOR CONSIDERATION

1. Wilberforce, the great English opponent of the African slave trade, has expressed the lordship of Christ in comprehensive terms. Reflect on the relationship between the season of Lent and the unlimited range of sanctification to which we have been called and which the risen Christ, through the Holy Spirit, has provided.

_____

_____

_____

_____

_____

_____

_____

2. What should happen in the secular dimensions of our lives once the new "controlling principle" of life has been enthroned? Does life in the world become less important? Study the life of Wilberforce for an answer.

_____

_____

_____

_____

_____

_____

_____


3. Wilberforce says Christians are "sworn enemies of sin and hold no conference with it." Why then does 1 John say, "If we say we have no sin, we deceive ourselves, and the truth is not in us. If we confess our sins, he is faithful and just, and will forgive our sins and cleanse us from all unrighteousness. If we say we have not sinned, we make him a liar, and his word is not in us" (1 John 1:8-10). Does 1 John refute Wilberforce?

_____

_____

_____

_____

_____

_____

_____

_____

# Saturday

## FEBRUARY 24, 2024

## READING FOR THE DAY

"Our Father, who art in the heavens." When you pray, it doesn't matter at all where heaven is. God is everywhere. It is said that where a king is present, his entire court is there. Wherever God is present, heaven is present, for wherever God's majesty is present, so is the fullness of his glory. Remember that Saint Augustine tells of seeking God in many places and eventually finding God in himself.

It is no small matter that we who are so easily distracted need to learn this. To commune with the eternal Father, to take delight in him, it isn't necessary to speak in a loud voice as though God were far removed. No matter how quietly we speak, our Father will hear us. We don't need wings to go searching for him; we need no more than a quiet place to be alone and to recognize his presence. Nor should we feel strange in the presence of so kind a Guest. We must speak to our Father very humbly, as we would to a kind earthly father. And we should petition him as we would our earthly father, tell him our troubles, and beg him to make them right. But after all has been said, we must recognize that we are unworthy to be called the Father's children.

Teresa of Ávila (1515-82), *The Way of Perfection*, chap. 28

## PRAYER

ALMIGHTY AND EVERLASTING GOD, you called us in Christ to love and unity; we pray that you will so rule our hearts by the Holy Spirit that we, being delivered by true fear of God from all fear of man, may evermore serve you in righteousness, mercy, humility, and gentleness toward each other, through your dear Son, our Redeemer, Jesus Christ. Amen.

Christian Charles J. Bunsen (1791–1860), *Prayers from the Collection of the Late Baron Bunsen*

## FOR REFLECTION

Job 11:7-9; Pss. 19:1-4; 139:1-24; Isa. 43:2; 57:15; Jer. 23:24; Matt. 6:1-13; 18:20; Rom. 8:38-39; Heb. 4:12-16; 13:12-16; 1 Pet. 5:6-11

## QUESTIONS FOR CONSIDERATION

1. Teresa of Ávila encourages us to recognize the presence of God in the ordinary avenues of life. Consider the ordinary dimensions of your life in which you need to more regularly recognize God's presence.

_____

_____

_____

_____

_____

_____

_____

_____

2. Part of practicing God's presence involves recognizing individual gifts for life and service. Where in your life do you discern such gifts?

_____

_____

_____

_____

_____

_____

_____


3. At midlife, Brother Lawrence (early seventeenth century) entered a monastery in Paris where he became the cook. Fifteen years later, he switched to the sandal repair shop. In both activities he learned to practice the presence of God by continually conversing with God. He said the worst that could happen was to lose the sense of God's presence. Reflect on how to practice the presence of God in your own "sandal repair shop." What is the role of the Holy Spirit in this process?

_____

_____

_____

_____

_____

_____

_____

# Second Sunday in Lent

## READING FOR THE DAY

Worship will never end; whether there be buildings, they will crumble; whether there be committees, they will fall asleep; whether there be budgets, they will add up to nothing. For we build for the present age, we discuss for the present age, and we pay for the present age; but when the age to come is here, the present age will be done away. For now we see the beauty of God through a glass, darkly, but then face to face; now we appreciate only part, but then we shall affirm and appreciate God, even as the living God has affirmed and appreciated us. So now our tasks are worship, mission and management, these three; but the greatest of these is worship.

. . . Worship is nothing more or less than love on its knees before the beloved; just as mission is love on its feet to serve the beloved.

N. T. Wright (1948– ), *For All God's Worth*, p. 9

# PRAYER

O LORD GOD, great, eternal, wonderful in glory, who makes and keeps covenant, who is Creator and Redeemer, the Help of all who flee to you, the Hope of all who cry to you, we worship you. "Holy, Holy, Holy is the LORD of hosts; the whole earth is full of [your] glory." Heal our waywardness and rebuke our inattention; by the aid of your grace, enable us to present ourselves as living sacrifices, holy and acceptable to you as our true and joyous worship, in the name of the Father, Son, and Holy Spirit. Amen.

Adapted from Introductory Prayers, in *Ancient Collects and Other Prayers*, p. 2; Isa. 6:3

## FOR REFLECTION

Exod. 15:2; 1 Chron. 16:29; Pss. 24:3-6; 29:2; 95:1-6; 96:9; Isa. 6:3; 40:21-23, 28-31; Hab. 2:18-20; Matt. 4:10; Rom. 12:1; Heb. 12:28; 13:15; Rev. 4:11; 15:3-4

## QUESTIONS FOR CONSIDERATION

1. The season of Lent provides us an opportunity to consider the meaning of the worship of God. Reflect on the distinction, though not rigid, between praise and worship. We worship God for *who he is*. We praise God for all *he has done*.

_____

_____

_____

_____

_____

_____

_____

_____

_____

_____

_____

_____

_____

2. Reflect on the danger of worshipping God only for what he has done for us.

_____

_____

_____

_____

_____

_____

_____

_____

_____

_____

_____

_____

_____

3. Lent is a time to examine our lives and ask the Holy Spirit to cleanse us from all that is idolatrous. The ancient Hebrews were tempted to elevate created things to the realm of worship. What form does that temptation assume today?

_____

_____

_____

_____

_____

_____

_____

_____

_____

_____

_____

_____

_____

_____

_____

_____

_____

# DAY 11
## Monday
### FEBRUARY 26, 2024

## READING FOR THE DAY

Do not Christians in many ways offend against the "law of faith," the "law of love"? In one sense we do not if our dispositions, words, and works spring from love. But in another sense we do and will more or less continue as long as we live. Neither love nor the power of the Holy Spirit makes us infallible; through unavoidable defect of understanding we cannot but err in many things. And these errors will frequently result in something wrong, in our disposition, words, and actions.

The holiest of Christians always need Christ as their *Prophet*, as "the light of the world." He gives them light moment by moment; the instant he withdraws, everything becomes darkness. Christians always need Christ as their *King*, for God does not give them a stock of holiness. Unless they receive the redeeming work of Christ moment by moment, nothing but sin should remain. Christians always need Christ as their *Priest*, to make atonement for them. Even perfect love is acceptable to God only through Jesus Christ. You are my light, my holiness, my heaven. Left to myself, I would be nothing but sin, darkness, and hell.

John Wesley (1703-91), *A Plain Account of Christian Perfection*, sec. 25

## PRAYER

GRACIOUS LORD, we entreat your mercy with our whole heart, that as you defend us against things adverse to the body, so you will set us free from the enemies of the soul. And as you grant us to rejoice in outward tranquility, grant to us your inward peace, through Jesus Christ our Lord. Amen.

Leonine Sacramentary (AD 440), *Prayers: Ancient and Modern*, p. 362

## FOR REFLECTION

Matt. 2:2; 11:27; 21:5; 27:11; Luke 22:42; John 8:12; 9:5; Eph. 5:2; 1 Tim. 2:1–5; Heb. 4:14–5:9; 6:20; 9:11-15; 1 John 1:5–2:6; Rev. 19:11

## QUESTIONS FOR CONSIDERATION

1. John Wesley was well known for urging Christians onward to the *entire sanctification* of their lives by the Holy Spirit. Yet here he makes clear that *sanctification* is a lifelong process. Reflect on the relationship between these two *complementary* dimensions of sanctification.

_____

_____

_____

_____

_____

_____

_____

_____

2. Reflect on the danger of putting so much trust in the progress we have made as Christians that we fail daily to live by grace through faith alone.

_____

_____

_____

_____

_____

_____

_____

_____

_____

3. Reflect on how confession of our failures as Jesus's people is itself an expression of faith and our love for God.

_____

_____

_____

_____

_____

_____

_____

_____

_____

_____

# DAY 12
## *Tuesday*
### FEBRUARY 27, 2024

## READING FOR THE DAY

If by the power of the cross, and by faith in Christ, death has been trampled down, it must be evident before the tribunal of truth that none other than Christ himself is the reason. He alone displays the trophies of triumph over death. He alone forced death to forfeit its power. When in the morning the sun rises, is there any doubt that the sun drove away the darkness? Even so, after the Savior's manifestation in the flesh, and his death on the cross, Christians know why they should hold death in contempt. For them it is quite clear that their Savior reduced death to impotence.

Day by day the Savior displays his victory in his disciples. When one sees humans, weak by nature, not fearing death's corruption, who would be so foolish as not to see that Christ gives them the victory? He who watches a serpent being walked on, knowing its former venomous power, no longer doubts its death. Or who could see children making sport of a lion and doubt its death or immobilization? Even so, now that Christ's disciples make sport of death, let no one doubt that Christ defeated death and destroyed its corruption.

Athanasius (ca. AD 297–373), *On the Incarnation of the Word*, sec. 29

## PRAYER

George R. Woodward (1848–1934), Hymnary

## FOR REFLECTION

Rom. 8:28-39; 1 Cor. 15:1-11; Col. 3:1-17; 1 Pet. 1:3-11; 4:1-11

## QUESTIONS FOR CONSIDERATION

1. What is the relationship between freedom from the fear of death and our hope of the resurrection (see 1 Cor. 15:42-58)?

_____

_____

_____

_____

_____

_____

_____

_____

_____

2. Death threatens to bring about the loss of meaning. How does the hope of the resurrection overcome that threat?

_____

_____

_____

_____

_____

_____

_____

_____

_____

_____

_____

_____

3. How may our attitude toward death become either a
   witness to our faith or an impediment? Does "craving"
   physical life at all costs bear testimony to our trust in the
   resurrection?

_____

_____

_____

_____

_____

_____

_____

_____

_____

_____

# Wednesday

## FEBRUARY 28, 2024

## READING FOR THE DAY

Suppose a king were to find a poor maiden, clothed in rags. Suppose the king were to take away her soiled and ragged clothing, wash away her filth, and make her his partner? What if he were to give her a portion at his table? This is just what the Lord did when he found us wandering and stricken. He gave us the medicine of salvation, took away our garments disgraced by sin, and then clothed us with royal, heavenly garments—the garments of the triune God—all shining and glorious. He put a crown on our heads, marking us as his children. He treated us to the royal table of joy and gladness. This is the meaning and mystery of the gospel.

Therefore, let us recognize our nobility in Christ. He has exalted us to kingly dignity. We are a chosen generation, a royal priesthood, and a holy nation. The visible glory of an earthly king is perishable. But the kingdom and wealth of the gospel of Jesus Christ will never dim or pass away.

It is the faithful nature of grace to remind us that were it not for the coming of the Savior, we would still be the poor, ragged maiden deserted by the side of the road.

Macarius-Symeon (late fourth century AD), *Fifty Spiritual Homilies,*
homily 27, secs. 3-4

## PRAYER

PRAISE TO THE LORD, the Almighty, the King of creation!
O my soul, praise him, for he is your health and salvation!
Come, all who hear; brothers and sisters, draw near,
join me in glad adoration! Amen.

Joachim Neander (1680), trans. Catherine Winkworth (1863), Hymnary

## FOR REFLECTION

Rom. 7:23; 2 Cor. 3:4-6; 2 Tim. 4:6-8; 1 Pet. 2:4-10; Rev. 1:4-8;
5:10; 20:6

## QUESTIONS FOR CONSIDERATION

1. Christians are not meant to live in the past. But the season
   of Lent is an appropriate time to remember our life prior
   to the gift of new creation in Christ. Moses warned the
   Hebrews against thinking their victory was a result of
   their own righteousness (Deut. 9:4-5). Reflect on that old
   life from which God's grace alone has delivered you.

_____

_____

_____

_____

_____

_____

_____

_____

_____

2. Lent provides an opportunity to rid ourselves of all self-sufficiency before God and to recall that no one is beyond the power of God's transforming love and forgiveness. Pause and pray fervently for someone you might have been tempted to write off as beyond the reach of God's grace.

_____

_____

_____

_____

_____

_____

_____

_____

3. Jesus repeatedly confronted Pharisees who prided themselves over the distance between themselves and "sinners" such as Zacchaeus (Luke 19:1-10). Ask God's forgiveness for the "Pharisee" that lingers in your evaluation of yourself and others.

_____

_____

_____

_____

_____

_____

_____

_____

# Thursday

## FEBRUARY 29, 2024

## READING FOR THE DAY

How you have loved us, good Father, who did not spare your only Son, but delivered him up for the ungodly! How you have loved us, for he who thought it not robbery to be equal with you was nevertheless made subject even to death on the cross. He alone, over whom death had no power, had power to lay down his life and power to take it up again. He was, for us to you, both Victor and Victim, the Victor because he was willing to become the Victim. He was, for us to you, Priest and Sacrifice, Priest because of the Sacrifice. By serving us he made us to become your servants, and by new birth made us to be your children. Well then is my hope firmly established in him, that you will through him heal all my infirmities, for he now sits at your right hand and makes intercession for us. Were this not true I would despair. For many and great are my infirmities; but your medicine is stronger. We would have completely despaired, because we would have thought your Word too far removed from us had he not been made flesh of our flesh and dwelt among us.

Augustine (AD 354–430), Bishop of Hippo, *Confessions*,
bk. 10, chap. 43, sec. 69

## PRAYER

SHINE FORTH within our hearts the incorruptible light of
Thy knowledge, O Master, Lover of mankind, and open the
eyes of our mind to the understanding of . . . Thy Gospel;
instill in us also the fear of Thy blessed commandments,
that, trampling down all lusts of the flesh, we may pursue
a spiritual way of life, being mindful of and doing all that is
well-pleasing unto Thee. Amen.

John Chrysostom (ca. AD 347–407), *The Divine Liturgy of St. John
Chrysostom*, Orthodox.net

## FOR REFLECTION

Pss. 88:5; 103:3; John 1:14; Rom. 5:8; 8:32–39; 2 Cor. 5:14; 13:14;
Gal. 2:20; Phil. 2:6–8

## QUESTIONS FOR CONSIDERATION

1. What is the relationship between Lent and the stronger
   medicine to which Augustine refers?

_____

_____

_____

_____

_____

_____

_____

_____

_____

2. Chrysostom prays for "the fear of [God's] blessed commandments." Is he praying as a Christian should? Is there
   an appropriate fear of the Lord for Christians?

   _____

   _____

   _____

   _____

   _____

   _____

   _____

   _____


3. Lent offers an opportunity to dwell on what the incarnation of God in Jesus of Nazareth means, that the very Son
   of God willingly took on himself the form of a servant.
   How is Christ's incarnation instructive for your discipleship and witness today (Phil. 2:5-11; Heb. 2:10-13)?

   _____

   _____

   _____

   _____

   _____

   _____

   _____

   _____

   _____

# DAY 15
## Friday
### MARCH 1, 2024

## READING FOR THE DAY

That Christian athlete Paul, desiring that we not rest on how well we have lived in the past, says, "Forgetting those things that are behind, and reaching forth to those things that are before, I press toward the mark for the prize of the high calling." This is generally true of human life. A person is no better for having eaten yesterday if he cannot satisfy his hunger today. In the same way, the soul gains nothing by yesterday's virtue unless it is followed by a virtuous life today. It is not he who begins well, but he who ends well who comes to Christian perfection. That person is approved by God.

We are passing through snares and treading in perilous places. Let us not try to master the Christian life all at once. When you have gained mastery in one area, begin to wage war against another hurdle. Beware of overconfidence. Meet each temptation with patient endurance. Let us not be rash in speech, quarrelsome, or covetous of vain glory. Always be ready to learn and slower to teach. Finally, it is much better to speak of the lives of godly people than to always talk about the sins of others.

Basil the Great (AD 330-79), Letters, letter 42, secs. 1-2

## PRAYER

O ETERNAL AND MOST GRACIOUS GOD, prompt us to consider your bountiful mercies. Teach us to fear every approach of sin and to live with jealous attention to your will. Establish in us a constant assurance of your grace. Help us to fly to you at the approach of every temptation, assured that you will lift us up and keep us from falling. Grant this, O Father, for the sake of him who knows our infirmities—your Son, our Savior, Christ Jesus. Amen.

John Donne, *Devotions*, pt. 1, Prayer 1

## FOR REFLECTION

Prov. 6:5; Ezek. 18:24; Luke 14:28, 30; Phil. 3:13-14; Heb. 10:19-25; 12:1-13; Jude vv. 17-23; Rev. 2:3-22

## QUESTIONS FOR CONSIDERATION

1. Reflect on the many resources Christians have for pressing "toward the mark for the prize of the high calling of God in Christ Jesus" (Phil. 3:14, KJV).

_____

_____

_____

_____

_____

_____

_____

_____

2. Reflect on the obstacles in your life that threaten to obstruct your pressing "toward the mark."

_____

_____

_____

_____

_____

_____

_____

_____

_____

3. Why must we remember that we press forward by strengthening one another in the Lord, not as isolated pilgrims? Why is Paul's metaphor of the body so important in this regard (Rom. 12:3-8)?

_____

_____

_____

_____

_____

_____

_____

_____

_____

# Saturday

## MARCH 2, 2024

## READING FOR THE DAY

After our adoption as the children of God we can expect that the devil will plot against us more intensely and violently than ever. He will be envious as he beholds the newborn child of God journeying toward the heavenly city. Don't be surprised when the devil hurls fiery temptations against us. He will seek to rob us of our new adornment, just as he robbed Adam and Eve. When the devil attacks, we ought to repeat the words of the apostle, "As many of us as were baptized into Christ were baptized into his death." If we have been conformed to Christ's death, then the old sinful self has become a corpse, pierced through by the javelin of baptism. Let us command the devil to flee, for what he seeks is dead. Once, the old self was his ally, but no longer. It has been crucified with Christ. It can no longer lust for wealth, slander, or revile others. The new self has learned how to pass by the things of this world and hasten on to the things of heaven. In the same way Paul testifies that the world is crucified to him, and he to the world. This must be the defining disposition of those who have been born anew.

Gregory of Nyssa (d. ca. 394), *On the Baptism of Christ*

## PRAYER

EVER-LIVING GOD, Father of all mercies, may my wealth be to become rich in holy virtues so that by them I can serve you and please you in all truth. Give me holy virtues for the honor and glory of your name. Make me steadfast in a faith that works through love. May the faith my tongue confesses be manifest in holy conduct. Amen.

Anselm (1033–1109), Archbishop of Canterbury,
*Book of Meditations and Prayers*, meditation 18, sec. 90

## FOR REFLECTION

Num. 25:7-9; Ps. 119:11; Rom. 6:3; 12:21; 1 Cor. 10:11-13; 2 Cor. 5:11-15; Gal. 6:14; James 4:7-10; 1 Pet. 5:8-11

## QUESTIONS FOR CONSIDERATION

1. "This must be the defining disposition of those who have been born anew." Gregory of Nyssa has penned a towering description of Christian holiness, of Christian discipleship. Some parts of the church act and speak as though Gregory has set the goal too high. They privilege the continuing power of sin over the power of transformation. Has Gregory set the standard too high? If not, by what power and path can his description of Christian discipleship become the norm for you?

_____

_____

_____

_____

_____

_____

2. Many people dismiss the reality of the devil. The New Testament doesn't do this (1 Pet. 5:8; Eph. 4:27). In what areas of your life are you most subject to Satan's attacks?

_____

_____

_____

_____

_____

_____

3. Gregory of Nyssa says Satan will try to strip us of our Christian "adornment." What are our chief weapons against his efforts (Eph. 6:10-18)?

_____

_____

_____

_____

_____

_____

4. Lent is a good time to reflect on the conclusion of Anselm's prayer: "May the faith my tongue confesses be manifest in holy conduct."

_____

_____

_____

_____

_____

# Third Sunday in Lent

## READING FOR THE DAY

Although he is revealed to be God incarnate, Jesus Christ does not refuse the conditions of human existence. He hungers, toils, and thirsts in weariness. He flees those who want to kill him and prays when in trouble. He who as God has a sleepless nature nevertheless slumbers on a pillow. And he who came into the world to suffer nevertheless prays to have the cup of suffering pass from him. He who strengthens those who believe on him nevertheless sweats blood in agony. And he who knew what manner of person Judas was nevertheless is betrayed by him. And he who will himself judge the whole earth nevertheless was judged by Caiaphas, counted as nothing by Herod, and scourged by Pilate. And he at whose beckoning stand thousands of thousands and myriads of myriads of angels and archangels nevertheless was mocked by Roman soldiers. And he who created the heavens is yet fastened to a wooden cross. And he who said, "I have power to lay down my life, and I have power to take it again," nevertheless bows his head and gives up the ghost. And he who bountifully gives life to all nevertheless has his side pierced with a spear. And he who raises the dead nevertheless is wrapped in linen and laid in a tomb. And he, though himself the Resurrection and the Life, on the third day is raised by the Father.

Hippolytus of Rome (AD 170–235),
*Against the Heresy of One Noetus*, para. 18

## PRAYER

O LOVING WISDOM OF OUR GOD!
When all was sin and shame,
A second Adam to the fight
And to the rescue came. Amen.

John Henry Newman (1801-90), Hymnary

## FOR REFLECTION

Isa. 53:4; Matt. 17:5; 27:29; Luke 23:44-46; John 10:18; 11:51-52; 19:23-24, 28-37

## QUESTIONS FOR CONSIDERATION

1. We often speak of God's strength given to us. But Hippolytus of Rome details our Lord's freely accepted vulnerability. How does his vulnerability become our strength?

_____

_____

_____

_____

_____

_____

_____

_____

_____

2. How does the vulnerability of Christ equip us to accept our own humanity?

_____

_____

_____

_____

_____

_____

_____

_____

_____

_____

3. One of Paul's most challenging statements is that in his sufferings he completes "what is lacking in Christ's afflictions for the sake of his body, that is, the church" (Col. 1:24). If Jesus fully suffered on the cross, what could Christian suffering, including the persecuted church, possibly add to Jesus's suffering? (Hint: consider the way of discipleship [Matt. 5:11-12; 10:16-24; 18:5-21; 24:9-14; 25:31-46].)

_____

_____

_____

_____

_____

_____

_____

_____

_____

_____

_____

4. What a staggering paradox! "He who created the heavens
   is yet fastened to a wooden cross." Reflect on what could
   possibly make this paradox a reality.

_____

_____

_____

_____

_____

_____

_____

_____

_____

_____

# Monday

## MARCH 4,· 2024

### READING FOR THE DAY

Nothing so quickly subverts Christian fortitude than becoming enamored with this world's goods. Often when Satan and his hosts are being put to flight, a Christian warrior is defeated because he permits himself to be diverted and infatuated by the enemy's spoils. If a Christian warrior abandons the fight and begins to plunder the enemy's booty, he will end up bringing Satan back to the battle after he had fled the field, and the Christian warrior may die among those he should have vanquished.

Fortitude, then, must repulse, must crush, the foul plague of being attracted to Satan's wares. They must hold no attraction for us. True virtues remain faithful to themselves. Fortitude should wage war on vices as though they were trying to poison virtue. But in doing so, fortitude must guard against self-glory.

Did holy Job lack any of this? He correctly assessed the dangers that menaced his safety and never permitted greed or the desire for pleasures or lusts to arise in his heart. He retained his trust in God. Job would not let vice accompany virtue.

Ambrose (ca. AD 340-97), Bishop of Milan, *On the Duties of the Clergy*, bk. 1, chap. 39, secs. 203-4

# PRAYER

> BREATHE ON ME, BREATH OF GOD
> Fill me with life anew,
> That I may love what thou dost love,
> And do what thou wouldst do. Amen.

Edwin Hatch (1835-89), Hymnary

## FOR REFLECTION

1 Kings 11:1-13; 2 Kings 5:1-27; Luke 12:35-38, 42; Eph. 6:11-17; Phil. 3:12–4:1; 2 Tim. 4:9-10; James 3:13–4:10

## QUESTIONS FOR CONSIDERATION

1. Ambrose warns against abandoning the Christian fight against Satan and beginning to "plunder the enemy's booty." In practical terms, what does this mean? What are the dangers in your life and in the church?

\
\
\
\
\
\
\

2. Ambrose commends Job. What may we learn from Job about holding fast our faith in our faithful God?

\
\

_____

_____

_____

_____

_____

_____

_____

3. "Nothing," warns Ambrose, "so quickly subverts Christian fortitude than becoming enamored with this world's goods." Ambrose was writing in the fourth century. But his warning is eminently applicable today. One of the persistent threats to godliness is the sin of endless and unbridled consumerism, the unrecognized belief that we are what we possess, a message much of the commercial world wants us to believe. How are you guarding against this besetting sin? Where are you most vulnerable?

_____

_____

_____

_____

_____

_____

_____

_____

_____

## DAY 18

# Tuesday

## MARCH 5, 2024

### READING FOR THE DAY

Those who are fully committed to Christ have uprooted perverted pride and the leaven of impatience. Carnal pride is the beginning of every sin. Christ's disciples must expel their rebellious self-wills that spring from carnal pride. They must give free reign to divine grace. Instead of being ruled by pride, self-will, and impatience, Jesus's disciples must bear in their hearts the crucified Christ, must rejoice in his wounds, and must desire nothing above him.

There is no true Christian obedience without humility, and no humility without love. All this was modeled by our Lord. In humility before his Father, Christ willingly bore the shameful cross. Nails would not have been enough to hold the God-man; only love could have kept him there. Because Christ's disciples know all this, they should seek no joy apart from the crucified Christ. Even if they could gain eternal life, escape hell, attain holiness, and receive spiritual and material consolation without being crucified with Christ, they would reject it.

Because Jesus's disciples know that only love and obedience held him to the cross, in reciprocal love they should be ready to be clothed with his shame, for they have been invited to the table of the spotless Lamb and will settle for nothing less.

Oh, glorious fellowship! Who would not give himself to death a thousand times to gain it?

Catherine of Siena (1347-80), "To Monna Agnese, Who Was the Wife of Messer Orso Malavoti," in *The Letters of Catherine Benincasa*

## PRAYER

O LORD GOD ALMIGHTY, we beseech and entreat you to perfect within us your grace. Pour out through our hands the gift of your pity and compassion. Amen.

Adaeus and Maris, The Liturgy of the Blessed Apostles (ca. AD 150)

## FOR REFLECTION

Matt. 26:36-46; Luke 14:11; Acts 2:36; Rom. 12:3; 1 Cor. 1:23-25; 2 Cor. 11:30; Eph. 2:10-22; Phil. 2:3-11; Heb. 12:1-3

## QUESTIONS FOR CONSIDERATION

1. The season of Lent is a perfect time for the Holy Spirit to examine us to determine if "perverted pride and the leaven of impatience" have crept into our discipleship. What might the Holy Spirit teach you and the church in this regard?

_____

_____

_____

_____

_____

_____

_____

_____

2. "Seek no joy apart from the crucified Christ," counsels
Catherine of Siena. Is her plea unrealistic? Should all
Christian life be lived with the crucified Christ in view?

_____

_____

_____

_____

_____

_____

3. Catherine of Siena leads us to consider our Lord's conde-
scension (Phil. 2:5-11). To be united with Jesus Messiah,
what must be our disposition toward ourselves and our
Christian sisters and brothers?

_____

_____

_____

_____

_____

_____

_____

# DAY 19
## Wednesday
### MARCH 6, 2024

(Irenaeus warns against the fictions of the arrogant heretics.)

## READING FOR THE DAY

It is therefore better and more profitable to belong to the simple and unlettered class, and by means of love to attain nearness to God, than by imagining ourselves learned and skillful to be found among those who are blasphemous against God. They conjure up another God in place of God the Father. For this reason Paul said, "Knowledge puffs up, but love edifies." He did not mean to speak against a true knowledge of God, for in that case he would have accused himself, but because he knew that some people, puffed up by a pretense of knowledge, fall away from loving God. They imagine they are perfect. That is why they set forth an imperfect Creator. It is for the purpose of rebuking such pride that Paul said, "Knowledge puffs up." It is therefore better that one should have no knowledge whatsoever of why a single thing in creation exists and still believe in God, and continue in his love, than to be puffed up with false knowledge and fall away from God's love, which is our life. It would be better that we search after no knowledge other than knowledge of Jesus

Christ the Son of God, who was crucified for us, than by subtle questions and hairsplitting speculations fall into impiety.

Irenaeus (ca. AD 130–ca. AD 202), *Against Heresies*, bk. 2, chap. 26, sec. 1

## PRAYER

> JESUS CALLS US: by your mercies,
> Savior, may we hear your call,
> Give our hearts to your obedience,
> Serve and love you best of all. Amen.

Cecil F. Alexander (1818-95), Hymnary

## FOR REFLECTION

Deut. 13:1-18; Acts 15:24; 1 Cor. 8:1; 2 Cor. 11:1-4; Gal. 1:6-12; Titus 3:10-11; 2 John vv. 10-11; Jude vv. 3-16

## QUESTIONS FOR CONSIDERATION

1. What resources do we have for detecting and opposing heresy in Christ's church? Whose responsibility is it to detect and oppose heresy? How?

2. Irenaeus has identified a major temptation many Christians have faced through the centuries: carnal pride over what we know. What is the difference between true Christian knowledge that "edifies" and knowledge that "puffs up"?

_____

_____

_____

_____

_____

_____

_____

_____

_____

3. According to Irenaeus, what is the proper role for education in all things Christian? Is diligent education in matters religious and secular an opponent of Christian faith?

_____

_____

_____

_____

_____

_____

_____

_____

_____

DAY 20

# Thursday

## MARCH 7, 2024

(Athenagoras responds to accusations against Christians
that they are perpetrators of many crimes.)

## READING FOR THE DAY

The lives of Christians are directed toward God as their rule,
so that each one among us may be blameless and irreproach-
able before him. We will not entertain even the thought of
the slightest sin. For if we believed that we should live only
the present life, then we might be suspected of sinning,
being enslaved to the flesh and blood, or mastered by gain
and carnal desire. But we know that God is witness to what
we think and what we say, both by night and by day, and that
he, being himself light, sees all things in our hearts.

We are persuaded that when we are removed from the present
life, we shall live another life, better than the present one, and
heavenly, not earthly (since we shall abide near God and with
God, free from all change or suffering in the soul). For these
reasons it is unlikely that we should choose to do evil or deliver ourselves over to the great Judge to be punished.

Athenagoras (ca. AD 133-ca. AD 190), *A Plea for the Christians*, chap. 31

# PRAYER

APPROACH, MY SOUL, the mercy seat,
Where Jesus answers prayer;
There humbly fall before his feet,
For none can perish there.

Thy promise is my only plea,
With this I venture nigh;
Thou callest burdened souls to thee,
And such, O Lord, am I. Amen.

John Newton (1725–1807), Hymnary

## FOR REFLECTION

Rom. 8:1-16; 1 Cor. 15:13-20, 34-58; 1 John 3:1-11

## QUESTIONS FOR CONSIDERATION

1. Romans accused the early Christians of crimes such as
   cannibalism (e.g., eating Christ's flesh). Today, what are
   accusations to which Christians must respond?

   _____

   _____

   _____

   _____

   _____

   _____

   _____

   _____

2. What timeless defense against accusations hurled at Christians does Athenagoras commend for Christians today?

_____

_____

_____

_____

_____

_____

_____

_____

_____

3. In what way should the Christian hope of Christ's return and the resurrection hold us steady in an accusatory world?

_____

_____

_____

_____

_____

_____

_____

_____

_____

_____

# DAY 21
## Friday
### MARCH 8, 2024

## READING FOR THE DAY

What sober-minded person, then, will not acknowledge that
we are not atheists? We worship the Creator of the universe.
We declare as we have been taught that God has no need for
streams of blood, libations, and incense. Through prayer
and thanksgiving we praise him for all things he has given.
We have been taught that the honor worthy of God is not to
consume by altar fires what he has given but to use it for
ourselves and for those in need. With gratitude we offer our
thanks to God. Through prayers and hymns we thank him
for our creation, for health, for the qualities of various kinds
of things, and for the changing seasons. In faith we place
before him petitions for our resurrection to incorruption. Our
teacher of all these things is Jesus Christ. He was born for
this purpose and was crucified under Pontius Pilate in the
times of Tiberius Caesar. We justifiably worship him, having
learned that he is the Son of the true God. Our accusers say
that our madness consists in calling a crucified man the Son
of the unchangeable and eternal God, the Creator of all.

The *First Apology* of Justin Martyr (ca. AD 100-ca. AD 165), chap. 13

## PRAYER

LOVE DIVINE! WHAT HAST THOU DONE!
The immortal God hath died for me!
The Father's coeternal Son
Bore all my sins upon the tree;
The immortal God for me hath died!
My Lord, my Love is crucified. Amen.

*A Collection of Hymns for the Use of the People Called Methodists* (1889),
hymn 28

## FOR REFLECTION

Ezra 9:5-8; Pss. 76:11; 96:8; Mark 8:27-33; 9:2-9; 1 Cor. 1:17-31;
Rev. 14:7; 19:10

## QUESTIONS FOR CONSIDERATION

1. Why did the Greeks and Romans accuse the early Christians of being atheists?

_____

_____

_____

_____

_____

_____

_____

2. In what way should the season of Lent promote true worship and remaining alert to the danger of idolatry in our lives?

_____

_____

_____

_____

_____

_____

_____

3. Idolatry seems to be a persistent problem among humans. In your culture, what are some of the prominent forms of idolatry? Are you tempted by any of these?

_____

_____

_____

_____

_____

_____

4. In the ancient world, among the Babylonians and other cultures, food was daily offered to idols because the people believed the idols became hungry. Today, "idols" must still be "fed." In your culture, how are idols fed?

_____

_____

_____

_____

_____

# DAY 22
## Saturday
### MARCH 9, 2024

## READING FOR THE DAY

"Hear now," said the shepherd, "how wicked is the action of anger, and in what way it overthrows the servants of God and turns them away from righteousness. But it does not act on those who are full of faith, nor does it turn them away from righteousness, for the power of the Lord is in them. Anger turns away the thoughtless and doubting. For as soon as it sees such people, it throws itself into their hearts, and for nothing at all the person becomes embittered on account of occurrences in life, maybe because of food, some super-fluous word that has been spoken, some friend, some gift or debt, or some such senseless affair. For all these things are foolish and empty and unprofitable to the servants of God. But patience is great, mighty, strong, and calm in the midst of great increase, joyful, rejoicing, free from care, glorifying God at all times, having no bitterness in her, and abiding in the Lord continually, meek and quiet. Depart from anger—that most wicked spirit—and you will be found in company with the purity the Lord loves."

The *Shepherd of Hermas* (second century), bk. 2, commandment 5

## PRAYER

DELIVER THE CAPTIVE; rescue the distressed; feed the hungry; comfort the fainthearted; convert the erring; enlighten the darkened; raise the fallen; confirm the wavering; heal the sick; and guide them all, good Lord, into the way of salvation and into your sacred fold. Deliver us from our iniquities; protect and defend us at all times. All glory, honor, adoration, and thanks are due to you, the Father, Son, and Holy Spirit, now, henceforth, and forevermore. Amen.

The Divine Liturgy of the Holy Apostle and Evangelist Mark (before AD 200)

## FOR REFLECTION

Matt. 5:22; Gal. 5:19-26; Eph. 4:26-27; Col. 3:8; Titus 1:7; James 3:11

## QUESTIONS FOR CONSIDERATION

1. The Bible speaks of God's anger (Deut. 9:8; Num. 11:1-2; Lam. 2:2). Why is God's anger justified and human anger condemned?

_____

_____

_____

_____

_____

_____

_____

_____

2. For Christians, is there a proper role for anger? If so, identify it.

_____

_____

_____

_____

_____

_____

_____

_____

_____


3. The *Shepherd of Hermas* warns against anger "throw[ing] itself into [our] hearts." Are there trip wires for spiritually harmful anger in your life that need to be addressed by self-examination and by the Holy Spirit?

_____

_____

_____

_____

_____

_____

_____

_____

_____

_____

# Fourth Sunday in Lent

(This reading describes the martyrdom of Polycarp as
recounted in a letter written by the church in Smyrna
to the church in Philomelium, a city of Phrygia.
Copies were to be sent to all the churches.)

## READING FOR THE DAY

Once the wild beasts had finished destroying the martyr
Germanicus, the whole multitude, not satisfied by Germanicus's death, cried out, "Away with the Atheists; let Polycarp
be sought out!" His location divulged to the authorities by
tortured informants, Polycarp after praying, was brought to
the stadium. The Irenarch Herod tried to convince Polycarp
to save his life by sacrificing to Caesar. Polycarp refused.

As he was brought forward, the crowd became tumultuous.
The proconsul asked, "Are you Polycarp?" Confessing that he
was, the proconsul tried to persuade Polycarp to deny Christ.
"Have respect to your old age. Swear by the genius of Caesar.
Say, 'Away with the atheists [i.e., the Christians].'" But Polycarp, gazing with a stern countenance on the entire multitude, and waving his hand toward them, said, "Away with
the Atheists!" Then the proconsul urged him, "Swear, and I
will set you at liberty, reproach Christ." Polycarp answered,

"Eighty and six years have I served him, and he never did me any injury: how then can I blaspheme my King and my Savior?"

*The Martyrdom of Polycarp* (ca. AD 69–ca. AD 155), chaps. 1–9

## PRAYER

O LORD, YOU ARE OUR GOD, who sets the captives free, who lifts up the downtrodden. Pity, relieve, and restore every Christian soul that is afflicted or wandering. Fill our hearts with joy and gladness, that at all times, having all sufficiency, we may abound to every good work in Christ Jesus our Lord. All glory, honor, adoration, and thanksgiving are due to you, the Father, Son, and Holy Ghost, now, henceforth, and forevermore. Amen.

The Divine Liturgy of the Holy Apostle and Evangelist Mark (before AD 200)

## FOR REFLECTION

Matt. 24:9; Luke 9:24; Acts 6:8–7:60; Rev. 6:9-11

## QUESTIONS FOR CONSIDERATION

1. The Greek word for martyr (*martys*) means "witness." Are there forms of martyrdom in the world today that do not involve physical death?

_____

_____

_____

_____

_____

_____

_____

_____

_____

_____

2. Are your prayers and the prayers of your church regularly voiced for the persecuted church in China, Africa, the Middle East, and other places, or are they mostly limited to prayers for your physical ailments?

_____

_____

_____

_____

_____

_____

_____

_____

_____

3. Appeals from the powers of this world to deny Jesus Christ differ from age to age, place to place, and person to person. What are some of the major appeals and powers in your world?

_____

_____

# Monday

## MARCH 11, 2024

### READING FOR THE DAY

Cheap grace is the deadly enemy of our Church. . . .

Cheap grace means grace sold on the market like cheapjacks' wares. The sacraments, the forgiveness of sin, and the consolations of religion are thrown away at cut prices. . . . Grace without price; grace without cost! . . .

Cheap grace means grace as a doctrine, a principle, a system. It means forgiveness of sins proclaimed as a general truth. . . .

Cheap grace means the justification of sin without the justification of the sinner. . . .

. . . Cheap grace is grace without discipleship, grace without the cross, and grace without Jesus Christ, living and incarnate.

Costly grace is the treasure hidden in the field; for the sake of it a man will gladly go and sell all that he has. . . .

Costly grace is the gospel which must be sought again and again, the gift which must be asked for, the door at which a man must knock.

Dietrich Bonhoeffer, "Costly Grace," chap. 1 in *The Cost of Discipleship*, pp. 45-47

## PRAYER

O GOD OF GRACE: who has clearly taught us that we "are justified by . . . grace as a gift"—and "if it is by grace, it is no longer on the basis of works": In your mercy deliver us from a notion of "cheap grace," for our salvation cost your Son his life. Forbid that we ever speak of forgiveness or justification without pointing to the cross and inviting those who do not know him to surrender their lives to him who gave it all up for our sake, Jesus Christ our Lord and Savior. Amen.

The Very Reverend Frank F. Limehouse III, Rom. 3:24; 11:6

## FOR REFLECTION

Matt. 10:37; Mark 8:34–38; Luke 9:23; 14:25–35; 23:32–49; John 15:18–25; Rom. 3:24; 11:6; 12:1–2; Phil. 1:21; 3:7–8; 2 Pet. 2:17–22; Rev. 3:1–6, 14–22

## QUESTIONS FOR CONSIDERATION

1. After considering Bonhoeffer's call to "costly grace," what are the dangers of "cheap grace" in your life and in Christ's church?

_____

_____

_____

_____

_____

_____

_____

2. In 1945, Bonhoeffer paid for "costly grace" at the hands of Nazi executioners. What will "costly grace" cost you?

_____

_____

_____

_____

_____

_____

_____

3. "Cheap grace" often surfaces as moral laxity. In what guise or ways does "cheap grace" as moral laxity and compromise currently threaten the church of Jesus Christ?

_____

_____

_____

_____

_____

_____

4. From what sources can we learn and embrace the meaning of "costly grace"?

_____

_____

_____

_____

_____

_____

# Tuesday

## MARCH 12, 2024

## READING FOR THE DAY

God's love brings every good and banishes all evil. O fire of love, what do you accomplish in Christians? You purify them as gold is purified; then you transport them to the celestial country.

If I could articulate the love of God that fills my heart, all humans would be inflamed, however remote from God's love they might now be. Before I leave this life, just once, O Lord, let me speak of your love as I have experienced it. Let me tell of what your love requires of those who receive it.

O divine love, with your tenderness you can break a heart that is harder than stone or melt it like wax. O divine love, you make great men esteem themselves as the least of the earth, and the richest as the poorest. O divine love, you make the wisdom of this world look like foolishness. To the learned you give understanding that surpasses all their knowledge. O divine love, you accomplish the whole work of salvation, which we can neither understand nor initiate. O divine love, even if a human heart is almost void of love, one spark is enough to set it aflame, abandon everything, and follow you.

Catherine of Genoa (1447–1510), *Spiritual Dialogue*, pt. 3, chap. 5
(*The Life and Doctrine of Saint Catherine of Genoa*)

## PRAYER

O LORD, I give myself to you. I know not what I am fitted for but to make a hell of myself without you. O Lord! I desire to make this compact with you: I will surrender my sinful being into your hands. You alone can hide it in your mercy. Fill me completely with your love that enlightens all other loves. Amen.

Catherine of Genoa, *Spiritual Dialogue*, pt. 1, chap. 12
(*The Life and Doctrine of Saint Catherine of Genoa*)

## FOR REFLECTION

2 Sam. 22:1-51; Pss. 25:1-22; 42:5-11; 63:1-8; Isa. 12:1-6; 38:9-15; 43:1-21; John 14:15-31; 1 Cor. 1:18-31; Eph. 2:1-10; Rev. 5:1-10; 7:13-17

## QUESTIONS FOR CONSIDERATION

1. How might Catherine of Genoa's description of God's love provide the correct context for the season of Lent?

_____

_____

_____

_____

_____

_____

2. "I am fitted . . . to make a hell of myself without you," confesses Catherine to her Lord. Reflect on what you would be apart from God's love?

_____

_____

_____

_____

_____

_____

_____

_____

3. God's "love . . . enlightens all other loves," says Catherine. In your life and practice, what does this affirmation mean?

_____

_____

_____

_____

_____

_____

4. John says God's love and redemption are for everyone (John 3:16). What is your role in communicating God's desire, provision, and invitation?

_____

_____

_____

_____

_____

_____

# DAY 25
## Wednesday
### MARCH 13, 2024

## READING FOR THE DAY

Far be it from us, soldiers of Christ, who are making our way toward heaven, to perplex ourselves about this world. "No man that wars entangles himself with the affairs of this life." This is St. Paul's rule, to "die daily." Daily he had fewer ties to this world and a larger treasure in heaven. Do not think it difficult to imitate Paul or that it requires some miraculous gift. We may all be like him according to our place and measure of grace. Let us fix our eyes upon Christ our Savior. Consider the splendor and glory of his holiness. Let us pray that a love for holiness will be created in our hearts, and then in due time holy acts that fit our circumstances will follow. Don't be distressed over what those acts will be. And don't try to draw a fine line between what is sinful and what is permissible. Instead, look to Christ, and relinquish anything you believe he would have you abandon. If you love him deeply, do not quibble about what discipleship requires; just venture everything on Jesus. He bids those who would live highest to live the lowest.

John Henry Newman (1801-90), "The Duty of Self Denial," in
*Parochial and Plain Sermons*, sermon VII

## PRAYER

FROM YOUR HAND, O God, we are willing to receive everything. You reach it out, your mighty hand, and catch the wise
in their foolishness. You open it, your gentle hand, and satisfy with blessing everything that lives. And even if it seems
that your arm is shortened, increase our faith and our trust
so that we might still hold fast to you. Amen.

Adapted from Søren Kierkegaard (1813-55), "Every Good and Every Perfect
Gift Is from Above," in *Eighteen Upbuilding Discourses,* trans. Hong, p. 31

## FOR REFLECTION

Matt. 5:13-16; 7:24-29; 16:24; Luke 12:22-34; 14:25-35; John
15:1-7; 1 Cor. 15:31; 2 Cor. 7:1; Phil. 3:7-14; Col. 3:1-17; 2 Tim.
2:4; 1 Pet. 5:6-10

## QUESTIONS FOR CONSIDERATION

1. John Newman recognizes that too often we "perplex
   ourselves about this world." The season of Lent provides
   an excellent opportunity for recognizing ways this temptation threatens us. What forms does this temptation
   assume in your life?

_____

_____

_____

_____

_____

_____

_____

2. How may we practice a Christlike love for the world while developing "fewer ties to this world and a larger treasure in heaven," as John Newman advises?

_____

_____

_____

_____

_____

_____

_____

_____

_____

3. Christ "bids those who would live highest to live the lowest." How might your station in life provide a place for practicing John Newman's exhortation?

_____

_____

_____

_____

_____

_____

_____

_____

_____

# Thursday

## MARCH 14, 2024

## READING FOR THE DAY

I am working to guard my spirit. The human and the divine can be too easily confused with each other; constant *watch-fulness* is necessary. Otherwise, without being aware of what is happening we may walk according to our own human interest instead of the Spirit of God. This once happened to Moses. He asked, "You rebels, must we draw water from this rock?" Then in anger he struck the rock instead of speaking to it as God had instructed. But God is a jealous God. He will not share his glory with anyone else, even with a favored servant such as Moses. Moses was severely punished for assuming God's authority and angrily striking the rock in his own choosing and power. Oh, to stand upon the watchtower and examine ourselves in all our self-deceptive impulses and actions.

Thank God, through his abundant grace, the language of the soul can be attuned to the indwelling Lord.

Phoebe Palmer (1807-74), diary entry for October 13, 1872, Quoted in Richard Wheatley, *The Life and Letters of Mrs. Phoebe Palmer*, p. 89

## PRAYER

FATHER OF ALL MERCIES, we give you most humble and hearty thanks for all your goodness and loving-kindness to us and all people. We bless you for our creation, preservation, and all the blessings of this life; but above all for your inestimable love in the redemption of the world by our Lord Jesus Christ; for the means of grace and the hope of glory. May we show forth your praise, not only with our lips but by walking before you in holiness and righteousness all our days, through Jesus our Lord. Amen.

*Services for Congregational Worship*, p. 85

## FOR REFLECTION

Num. 20:1-13; Deut. 4:9; Ps. 39:1; Isa. 42:8; 48:9-13; Matt. 24:3-8; Luke 11:33-36; 12:15-21; Rom. 13:11-14; 1 Cor. 9:24-27; Eph. 5:15-20; 6:18-20

## QUESTIONS FOR CONSIDERATION

1.  Phoebe Palmer championed the holy life. Yet she was tempted to confuse the human with the divine. In what ways do you also face this danger?

_____

_____

_____

_____

_____

_____

_____

_____

2. How may we hope to distinguish between human interest and divine interest?

_____

_____

_____

_____

_____

_____

_____

_____

_____

3. In the book of Isaiah, we hear God say that he will not share his glory with any other (42:8). In what ways are we tempted to share God's glory with created things, including things of religious importance?

_____

_____

_____

_____

_____

_____

_____

_____

_____

# DAY 27

## Friday

### MARCH 15, 2024

## READING FOR THE DAY

A Christian is a *perfectly free Lord of all, subject to none*; a Christian *is the most dutiful servant of all, subject to everyone.* These statements appear contradictory. But if they agree with each other, they will explain the gospel very well.

Each Christian is by trust in Christ so exalted above dependence upon works that, by virtue of being redeemed by God's power, he is lord of all things. Nothing can rob him of the gift of salvation. All things are made subservient to trust in Christ. This does not mean that Christians are placed above all things to control them by physical power.

Insofar as a Christian is free from dependence upon works because he is redeemed by grace through faith alone, he does no works. He is a free lord of all things and possesses all things. But now that he is free from works as a means for obtaining salvation, he is servant of all; he does all kinds of works that fulfill the law. This is that faith that works through obedient love. It is the Christian's singular occupation to serve God and his neighbor joyfully and without thought of gain.

Martin Luther (1483–1546), *On the Freedom of a Christian*

## PRAYER

O LORD, make your law our delight. Plant in our hearts that love that fulfills the law. Teach us to love you with our entire will and being, and our neighbor as ourselves. Keep us from dividing your commandments into great and small, according to our own blind preferences. And give us grace humbly to receive, as you clearly taught us, that whoever transgresses in one point is guilty of the whole law. Amen.

Christina Georgina Rossetti (1830-94), *Prayers: Ancient and Modern*

## FOR REFLECTION

Rom. 8:1-4, 28; 13:8; 14:1-23; 1 Cor. 2:10-14; 3:21-23; 9:19; Gal. 5:1-6, 13-21; 1 Tim. 2:3-7; James 1:22-2:17; 1 Pet. 1:13-23; 2:1-25

## QUESTIONS FOR CONSIDERATION

1. If a Christians is "a perfectly free Lord of all, subject to none," what sense does it make to say, as Luther does, that a Christian is "the most dutiful servant of all, subject to everyone" (see Matt. 23:11)?

_____

_____

_____

_____

_____

_____

_____

_____

2. If we are saved by grace through faith alone, what role could "works" possibly play in our salvation? (Hint: see Gal. 5:6.)

_____

_____

_____

_____

_____

3. In what ways are Christians confronted with the danger of trusting in "works" as the source of their security in Christ?

_____

_____

_____

_____

_____

4. If faith is something we express, is it a work—that is, a human accomplishment offered to God?

_____

_____

_____

_____

_____

## DAY 28

# Saturday

## MARCH 16, 2024

## READING FOR THE DAY

The wisdom of God will make us like Christ if we experience "the power of his resurrection and the fellowship of his sufferings." For this is the heart of the apostles' teaching and the most holy "faith delivered to us," which even the unlearned can receive and which those of slight learning have taught to others. We do not give "heed to endless genealogies" but study rather to observe a straightforward course of life; lest, having been deprived of the Divine Spirit, we fail to attain to the kingdom of heaven. Truly the first thing is to deny oneself and to follow Christ. Those who do this are borne onward to perfection, having fulfilled their Teacher's will. They become children of God by spiritual regeneration and heirs of the kingdom of heaven. Those who seek the kingdom of heaven will never be forsaken.

Irenaeus (ca. AD 130–ca. AD 202),
*Fragments from the Lost Writings of Irenaeus*, no. 36

## PRAYER

COME, THOU, HOLY SPIRIT, come!
And from thy celestial home
  Shed a ray of light divine!
Come, thou Father of the poor!
Come, thou Source of all our store!
  Come, within our bosoms shine! Amen.

Unknown author (twelfth century AD), trans. Edward Caswall (1849),
Hymnary

## FOR REFLECTION

1 Cor. 1:11–31; Phil. 3:6–16; 1 Tim. 1:4; Heb. 2:1–3; Jude v. 3

## QUESTIONS FOR CONSIDERATION

1. The Christian faith values simplicity, even the simplicity
   of a child. Why is simplicity so important (Matt. 18:1–5)?

_____

_____

_____

_____

_____

_____

2. Understanding the Christian faith well requires lifelong
   study. As learning increases, is simplicity replaced?

_____

_____

_____

_____

_____

_____

_____

3. By Roman standards, the apostle Paul was highly ed-
   ucated, potentially well positioned in Roman culture.
   Instead, he placed everything in service to Jesus Christ.
   Can a Christian occupy a leading position in society, such
   as holding political office or becoming prominent in the
   sciences, and still place himself or herself primarily in
   service to Jesus Christ? If so, how?

_____

_____

_____

_____

_____

4. Along with Paul, Irenaeus warns against "endless genealogies," including endless "speculations" about the Bible
   and the Christian faith (see 1 Tim. 1:4). What forms do
   endless speculations assume in the church today?

_____

_____

_____

_____

_____

# Fifth Sunday in Lent

MARCH 17, 2024

## READING FOR THE DAY

There is no greater favor from God than sending his Word.
But what is this Word? The apostle Paul says the Word of God
is the gospel of God concerning his Son—incarnate, suffer-
ing, risen, and glorified through the Spirit, who sanctifies.
To preach Christ means to feed the soul, make it righteous,
set it free, and save it, provided it believes the preaching.
Faith alone is the saving and efficacious use of God's Word.
The Word of God cannot be received and honored by works
but by faith in Christ alone. Just as the soul needs the Word
alone for life and justification, it is justified by faith alone.
If it could be justified by works, it would have no need of the
Word or faith.

Faith cannot exist in connection with works. If you think
you could be justified by works in connection with faith, that
would involve halting between two opinions. The moment
you begin to trust Christ, you learn that everything in you
is completely blameworthy, sinful, and damnable. When you
have learned this, you will know that Christ the Word is absolutely necessary; he suffered and rose again so by faith you
may become a new person; your sins are forgiven, and you
are justified by the merits of Jesus Christ alone.

Martin Luther, *On the Freedom of a Christian*

## PRAYER

O ETERNAL GOD, we joyfully confess that our salvation and righteousness are founded entirely upon your eternal grace given to us through the person and office of the Lord Jesus Christ. We confess that in him alone we are made righteous, holy, alive, blessed, children and heirs of God. Amen.

Johann Arndt (1555–1621), *True Christianity,*
based on bk. 2, chap. 3, para. 10

## FOR REFLECTION

Hab. 2:4; Acts 2:14-38; Rom. 1:1-17; 3:10-12, 21-23; 10:4, 9; Gal. 3:1-14

## QUESTIONS FOR CONSIDERATION

1. Christians often speak of the Bible as the Word of God. The apostle Paul and Martin Luther speak of the gospel as the Word of God. John says Jesus Christ is the Word of God (John 1:1-5). What is the correct order and relationship between these three?

_____

_____

_____

_____

_____

_____

_____

_____

_____

_____

_____

2. Martin Luther says faith cannot exist in connection with works. Paul says the two are inseparable, that "faith work[s] through love" (Gal. 5:6). Are both of them correct?

_____

_____

_____

_____

_____

_____

_____

_____

_____

_____

_____

3. The season of Lent offers an opportunity to ask, "Having begun by grace through faith alone, do I continue to live by grace through faith alone, or has some additional 'source' crept into my life?" Identify some alien sources that threaten living by grace alone?

_____

_____

_____

# DAY 29

## *Monday*

### MARCH 18, 2024

## READING FOR THE DAY

The leading principle by which our Divine Master trains his people is that they should present themselves as a "living sacrifice, holy and acceptable to God, which is their reasonable service." We belong to God; therefore, let his wisdom and will preside over all our actions. O how great the faithfulness of the Christian who, having been taught that he is not his own, has surrendered dominion and governance of himself to God! Just as the surest path to destruction is for a person to make himself lord of his life, so the only haven of safety is to have no other will and no other wisdom than to follow the Lord wherever he leads.

Let this, then, be the first step toward holiness, to abandon ourselves and devote the whole energy of our minds to God's service, obeying not only in our words but also with minds cleansed from life according to the flesh. This is discipleship that freely obeys the call of the Holy Spirit. Philosophers assign governance of the self to reason. But Christ bids us submit to the Holy Spirit so that we no longer live but Christ lives and reigns in us.

John Calvin (1509-64), *Institutes of the Christian Religion*,
bk. 3, chap. 7, sec. 1

## PRAYER

O HOLY SPIRIT, we surrender to you all our members. Make them to be instruments of your righteousness. We bring to you our hearts, impure and blemished though they be; wash them in the blood of Christ, and sanctify them to be your temple wherein you reign. Fill us with living faith, grace, and love. May we live henceforward according to your Word and obey in all things your voice. May this be our true worship and thanksgiving. Amen.

Christian Charles J. Bunsen (1791–1860), *Prayers from the Collection of the Late Baron Bunsen*

## FOR REFLECTION

Rom. 8:3–11; 12:1–2; 14:8; Gal. 2:20; Eph. 4:23; Phil. 3:7–11; Titus 2:11–14; 1 Pet. 3:14–18

## QUESTIONS FOR CONSIDERATION

1. The season of Lent is an opportune time to listen carefully to John Calvin's appeal. If something has been sacrificed, how can it still live?

2. Calvin could be understood as eliminating reason from Christian faith. Must one abandon reason to become a Christian? Or does Calvin's statement have some other meaning?

_____

_____

_____

_____

_____

3. Calvin warns that "the surest path to destruction is for a person to make himself lord of his [own] life." Can this danger be eliminated once and for all, or must it be confronted regularly?

_____

_____

_____

_____

_____

4. Is it God's desire to destroy the human will, human freedom, the self, as some religious leaders have taught? Is that the correct meaning of "self-sacrifice" or "death to self"?

_____

_____

_____

_____

_____

DAY 30

# Tuesday

## MARCH 19, 2024

(Thomas Cranmer's Summary of the
Gospel and Christian Life, Part 1)

## READING FOR THE DAY

Consider the infinite benefits God has mercifully shown
without our deserving them. He created us out of nothing and from his infinite goodness. Out of common clay he
formed us in his own image. Moreover, even when because
of our sins we were condemned to eternal punishment, he
gave his only begotten Son, being God Eternal, immortal and
equal to his Father in power and glory, to become incarnate
among us, to take our infirmities upon himself. In a full
humanity like as ours, Christ willingly suffered the most
shameful and painful death for our sins. He did all this to
justify us and restore us to life everlasting. He has made us
to be beloved children, brethren to his only Son, our Savior, and inheritors of his eternal kingdom. These great and
merciful benefits do not prompt us to be idle, but they move
us to present ourselves to God completely, to serve him in all
good deeds, obeying his commandments, and seeking in all
things to glorify him. God's benefits move us for his sake to

be ready to give ourselves to our neighbors and as much as is within our power to do good to all persons.

Thomas Cranmer (1489–1556), "Homily of Salvation," in *The Works of Thomas Cranmer*, vol. 2, p. 134

## PRAYER

O LORD, mercifully receive the prayers of your people who call upon you, and grant that they may know and understand what things they ought to do, and also may have grace and power faithfully to accomplish them; through Jesus Christ our Lord, who lives and reigns with you and the Holy Spirit, one God, now and for ever. Amen.

"Proper 10," Collects: Contemporary, in BCP

## FOR REFLECTION

Gen. 1:26–31; 2:5–9; Pss. 136:1–9; 146:1–9; 147:5–11; Matt. 5:14–20; 18:1–22; John 15:1–20; Rom. 12:1–21; 1 Cor. 15:1–11; 2 Pet. 1:3–18; 1 John 3:1–4

## QUESTIONS FOR CONSIDERATION

1. Point by point, join with Thomas Cranmer—pivotal shaper of Anglican piety, worship, and theology—as he rehearses our riches in Christ Jesus.

_____

_____

_____

_____

_____

_____

2. The selected collect (the gathering of the people together) from the Book of Common Prayer petitions God not only to teach us what we ought to do but also to grant grace and power to *enact* what we are taught. Reflect on the power of God's grace that enables Christians to obey God's will as celebrated by the apostle Paul in Ephesians 1:15-23.

_____

_____

_____

_____

_____

_____

_____

_____

3. Reflect on what Cranmer says about how the "great and merciful benefits" of God's grace should prepare Christians to live.

_____

_____

_____

_____

_____

_____

_____

_____

_____

# Wednesday

## MARCH 20, 2024

## READING FOR THE DAY

Jesus Christ "fills out" the "I Am" of God—rest for the weary, peace for the storm tossed, strength for the weak, wisdom for the foolish, righteousness for the sinful. It is our privilege and duty to reject all concepts of God that conflict with the blessed life, character, and teaching of Jesus. But you might say, "Ah yes, this is all true, but how can I take hold of it? I am a poor, unworthy creature. I dare not believe such a fullness of grace belongs to me." How can you take hold of it? You can't at all! But you can let it take hold of you. It is magnificent good news. Do with it as you would any reliable earthly good news. Take your stand on Christ's trustworthiness. Say, "I am going to believe right straight through." All that he is, God is. I can never again be frightened of God as though he were a hard taskmaster who makes demands as a removed and unapproachable deity, wrapped in his own splendor, indifferent to my sorrows and fears. Embrace no thought of God at variance with Christ, and your life will be transformed.

Hannah Whitall Smith (1832–1911), *The God of All Comfort*, chap. 2

## PRAYER

O GOD, who by your dear Son has consecrated unto us a new
and living way into your presence, grant to us, we beseech
you, the assurance of your mercy, and sanctify us by your
heavenly grace; that we, approaching you with a pure heart
and undefiled conscience, may offer unto you a sacrifice in
righteousness and celebrate your blessed name in the faith
and spirit of your Son. Amen.

*Services for Congregational Worship, p. 17*

## FOR REFLECTION

Exod. 3:1-14; John 1:15-18; 5:31-47; 8:48-59; 10:11-18; 11:25-26;
Rom. 3:21-26; 5:1-11; 8:28-39; Phil. 4:8-9; Heb. 4:14-16; 5:7-8;
1 John 5:18-21

## QUESTIONS FOR CONSIDERATION

1. Hannah Whitall Smith has stated a truth absolutely central to Christian faith: everything we say about God must
   be cleared through the person and work of Jesus Christ.
   Do you have questions about God that need to be cleared
   through Jesus Christ?

---

---

---

---

---

---

---

2. Can you think of one or two things you encounter in the Old Testament that need to be cleared through Jesus Christ?

_____

_____

_____

_____

_____

3. One of the most prominent attributes of God affirmed in the Old Testament is his "steadfast love" (*hesed*; see Deut. 5:10; Isa. 54:8, 10; 55:3; 63:7–9; Jer. 9:24; Jon. 4:2). Reflect on how this attribute is most completely expressed in and by Jesus. Read what the apostle Paul says about Jesus and the promises of God (2 Cor. 1:19–22).

_____

_____

_____

_____

_____

4. Occasionally, Christians mistakenly speak of God the Father as observing Jesus's death from a distance. If Jesus is the supreme manifestation and presence of the triune God, does the Father at any point distance himself from his suffering Son, or does he suffer in and with his Son?

_____

_____

_____

_____

# Thursday

## MARCH 21, 2024

## READING FOR THE DAY

Those who, through the Divine Word, plant and cultivate
the virtues that reflect "the Firstborn of all creation" raise
statues in worship of Christ their prototype. He is the "the
image of the invisible God," God the Only Begotten. Those
who put away their old self, corrupt and deluded by lust,
and are clothed with the new self, created according to the
likeness of God in true righteousness and holiness, take on
themselves the very image of him who created them. They
raise within themselves a statue such as the Most High God
desires.

By contemplating God with a pure heart, Christians become
imitators of Christ. The statues they strive to raise are not
those of a lifeless and senseless kind. They are not raised
to house greedy spirits bent on doing evil things. Instead,
Christians are filled with the Spirit of God, who dwells in
them. The Spirit takes his abode in those who are being
transformed in Christ's image.

Origen (ca. AD 185–ca. AD 254), *Against Celsus*, bk. 8, chaps. 17, 18

## PRAYER

ALMIGHTY GOD, Father of all mercies, we pray, give us
such an awareness of your mercies, that with truly thankful hearts we may show forth your praise, not only with our
lips but in our lives, by giving up ourselves to your service
and by walking before you in holiness and righteousness all
our days; through Jesus Christ our Lord, to whom, with you
and the Holy Spirit, be honor and glory throughout all ages.
Amen.

"The General Thanksgiving," Daily Evening Prayer: Rite Two, in BCP

## FOR REFLECTION

John 15:1-5; Rom. 5:1–6:14; 8:1-6; 2 Cor. 4:1-7; Eph. 4:22-24

## QUESTIONS FOR CONSIDERATION

1. The season of Advent and the season of Lent provide
   opportunities for Christians to consider why they worship Jesus Christ as God. Does worship of Christ endanger
   monotheism—that is, worship of one God alone?

_____

_____

_____

_____

_____

_____

_____

_____

2. Why did Jesus's first followers feel compelled to use "Jesus language" when speaking of God? (See Phil. 2:5–11 and Col. 1:15–20 for two answers.)

_____

_____

_____

_____

_____

3. Old Testament scholar John Walton explains that for the Hebrews, people are the image of God because they embody God's qualities and do God's work. They are symbols of his presence and act on his behalf as his representatives.[4] Use Walton's explanation to reflect on Origen's statement that those clothed with the new self in Jesus Christ "take on . . . the very image of him who created them."

_____

_____

_____

_____

_____

4. Origen says Christians must "cultivate the virtues that reflect 'the Firstborn of all creation.'" Search the New Testament to identify five or more of those virtues.

_____

_____

_____

_____

# DAY 33

## Friday

### MARCH 22, 2024

## READING FOR THE DAY

Can one prove from history that Christ was God? Asked another way, is it not absurd for a person to try to prove that Christ is God? Asserting that a human is God is at variance with human reason.

The "proofs" given in Scripture for the deity of Christ, such as the miracles and Jesus's resurrection are apprehended by faith, not by reason unenlightened by the Holy Spirit. But someone might ask, Has not the church worshipped Christ for eighteen hundred years? Does this not prove his deity? Has not history step-by-step verified Christ's deity? No! In all eternity, the best that history can do is to prove that Jesus was a great man, maybe the greatest.

Do not dress Jesus in brilliant proofs that remove the stumbling block—faith, God's gift. Only the Father in heaven can, through the gift of faith, reveal that in Christ's debasement he was God incarnate and that he will return in glory. The shabby rational proofs are blasphemous because they displace faith.

Søren Kierkegaard, "The Pause," in *Preparation for a Christian Life [Training in Christianity]*, in *Selections*, trans. Hollander, pp. 167-71

## PRAYER

O GOD, . . . Thou art always and invariably to be found, and always to be found unchanged. Whether in life or in death, no one journeys so far afield that Thou art not to be found by Him. . . . And whenever any human being comes to Thee, . . . if he comes in sincerity he always finds Thy love equally warm, like a spring's unchanged coolness, O Thou who art unchangeable! Amen!

Søren Kierkegaard, "The Unchangeableness of God," in *Edifying Discourses: A Selection*, ed. Holmer, p. 265

## FOR REFLECTION

Luke 24:28-35; John 1:10-13; 3:1-6; 6:10-71; 15:1-27; 20:19-24; Rom. 10:9-10; 1 Cor. 2:5; Gal. 2:20; Eph. 2:8

## QUESTIONS FOR CONSIDERATION

1. During his brief adult life, Søren Kierkegaard battled superficial Christianity in his native Denmark. He struggled against those who wanted to make the Christian faith "reasonable" and easily accessible. They wanted discipleship to be something that fit neatly into the surrounding culture. In what forms do we still battle these enemies of true Christian faith and discipleship?

_____

_____

_____

_____

_____

_____

2. Kierkegaard said that the Christ who can be consigned to ancient history and managed from a distance is no Christ at all. He said Jesus Christ must become our living and reigning contemporary. Reflect on the worthlessness of a Christ consigned to history.

_____

_____

_____

_____

_____

_____

_____

_____

_____

3. In what ways are we tempted to "dress Jesus in brilliant proofs" that remove the stumbling block of faith?

_____

_____

_____

_____

_____

_____

_____

_____

_____

# DAY 34
## Saturday
### MARCH 23, 2024

## READING FOR THE DAY

Pray without ceasing on behalf of others. For there is in them hope of repentance, that they may attain to God. See, then, that they be instructed by your works, if in no other way. Be meek in response to their wrath, humble in opposition to their boasting: to their blasphemies return your prayers; in contrast to their error, be steadfast in the faith; and for their cruelty, manifest your gentleness. While we take care not to imitate their conduct, let us be found their brethren in all true kindness; and let us seek to be followers of the Lord (who was ever more unjustly treated, more destitute, more condemned?) so that no plant of the devil may be found in you, but you may remain in all holiness and sobriety in Jesus Christ, both with respect to the flesh and the spirit.

Ignatius (d. ca. AD 107), *Epistle to the Ephesians*, chap. 10

## PRAYER

JOYFUL, JOYFUL, WE ADORE THEE,
    God of glory, Lord of love;
Hearts unfold like flow'rs before thee,
    Opening to the sun above.
Melt the clouds of sin and sadness;
    Drive the dark of doubt away.
Giver of immortal gladness,
    Fill us with the light of day! Amen.

Henry van Dyke (1852–1933), STTL, no. 17

## FOR REFLECTION

Num. 7:3; Ps. 34:1-10; Isa. 57:15; Jer. 8:4; Matt. 5:4, 13-16; Gal. 5:22; Col. 1:21-23; 2 Tim. 2:24-25; James 3:17; Rev. 2:8-11

## QUESTIONS FOR CONSIDERATION

1. The season of Lent is predominantly given to self-reflection and humility before God. Ignatius reminds us that prayer for the salvation of others should never escape our attention. In the Spirit's power, pray for those near you, perhaps family members, who do not yet know Jesus Christ as their Redeemer.

---

---

---

---

---

---

---

2. Ignatius's exhortation came during a time when the church was being persecuted by Romans and unbelieving Jews. Let us follow Jesus's instructions (Matt. 5:43–48) and Ignatius's model by praying for the salvation of those who oppose our Lord and who persecute his church.

_____

_____

_____

_____

_____

_____

_____

_____


3. Pray for the kind of life Ignatius says we must practice if we are to become effective witnesses for Jesus Christ: "that no plant of the devil may be found in you, but you may remain in all holiness and sobriety in Jesus Christ."

_____

_____

_____

_____

_____

_____

_____

_____

# Palm Sunday (Passion Sunday)

## READING FOR THE DAY

The "Sun of Righteousness" has changed sunset into sunrise and through the cross has brought death to life. And having wrenched humans from destruction, he has raised them to the skies, transforming mortality into immortality and translating earth to heaven. He, the Husbandman of God, has bestowed on us the truly great, divine, and inalienable inheritance of the Father. He sanctified us by heavenly teaching, putting his laws into our minds and writing them on our hearts. And though God needs nothing, let us render to him the grateful recompense of a thankful heart and of piety.

Let the light then shine in our hidden part, that is, the heart; and let the beams of knowledge arise to reveal and irradiate the hidden inner person, the disciple of him who is the Light, the friend and fellow heir of Christ. Especially now that we have come to know the most precious and venerable name of the good Father, who to a pious and good child gives gentle counsel and commands what is beneficial for his child.

Clement of Alexandria (ca. AD 150–ca. AD 215),
*Exhortation to the Heathen*, chap. 11

# PRAYER

THE DAY OF RESURRECTION!
Earth, tell it out abroad;
The Passover of gladness,
The Passover of God.
From death to life eternal,
From earth to the sky,
Our Christ has brought us over,
With hymns of victory. Amen.

John of Damascus (ca. AD 675–749), trans. John M. Neale (1862), Hymnary

## FOR REFLECTION

Jer. 31:31-34; Luke 1:68-79; John 12:42-50; 1 Cor. 15:53-54;
Eph. 1:3-8; 2:13-22; 5:8, 13; 1 Thess. 4:1-18; Heb. 8:10-12

## QUESTIONS FOR CONSIDERATION

1. Clement of Alexandria beautifully expresses what King
   Jesus will accomplish at the end of Holy Week: wrench
   "humans from destruction." However, today, on a humble
   donkey (Zech. 9:9), Jesus rides into a city that will reject
   him; his divine vision for Israel runs contrary to what
   most of the people expect. As we wave our palms and
   shout our hosannas today, do we welcome the one who
   actually arrives or do we require another kind of king?

_____

_____

_____

_____

_____

_____

_____

_____

_____

_____

_____

2. Luke says that as Jesus approached Jerusalem, he wept over it. Israel would reject God's "visitation" (19:44). In the person of Jesus, God had returned as promised to redeem his people and dwell in their midst. In AD 70, the Romans destroyed the city and the temple. What is the danger that we face today of missing Jesus's visitation?

_____

_____

_____

_____

_____

_____

_____

_____

_____

_____

_____

3. Luke says Jesus immediately entered the temple and drove "out those who sold" (19:45; see vv. 45-46) because they were abusing the place of worship. Christians are temples

"of the Holy Spirit" (1 Cor. 6:19). On this Palm Sunday, while reflecting on the irradiation or illumination of our temples, as Clement describes, let us invite Jesus to visit and examine our temples as he visited the Jerusalem temple long ago.

_____

_____

_____

_____

_____

_____

_____

_____

_____

_____

_____

DAY 35

# Monday of Holy Week

## MARCH 25, 2024

## READING FOR THE DAY

When the witness of the New Testament is taken as a whole, a deep consistency can be detected. . . . The "real Jesus" is . . . the powerful, resurrected Lord whose transforming Spirit is active in the community. But following Jesus is not a matter of the sort of power that dominates others, nor of "already ruling" in the kingdom of God. . . . It is instead a matter of transformation according to the pattern of the Messiah. The "real Jesus" is therefore also the one who through the Spirit replicates in the lives of believers faithful obedience to God and loving service to others. . . . Everywhere in these writings the image of Jesus involves the tension-filled paradox of death and resurrection, suffering and glory.

. . . Discipleship does not consist in a countercultural critique of society. Discipleship does not consist in working overwhelming miracles. . . . The pattern of obedient suffering and loving service is [normative].

Luke Timothy Johnson, *The Real Jesus*, p. 166

## PRAYER

ALMIGHTY AND EVERLASTING GOD, who adorns the sacred body of your church with the confessions of holy martyrs: Grant to us, we pray, both by their doctrines and their faithful examples a "genuineness of . . . faith, more precious than gold." May our faith be tested and refined, that it may redound to your honor and glory at the revelation of Jesus Christ. Mercifully increase our faith and ever fortify our discipleship, through the power of the Holy Spirit. Amen.

Adapted from "Saints Days," Prayers for Sacred Seasons, in Ancient Collects and Other Prayers, pp. 68-69; 1 Pet. 1:7

## FOR REFLECTION

Matt. 5:10; 28:16-20; John 7:27-44; 10:27-30; 14:1-7, 12-17; 16:12-15; 17:17-19; Acts 1:1-11; 2:1-4; Rom. 1:1-5; 8:1-8; 15:19; 1 Cor. 4:8; Phil. 1:27–2:3; 1 Pet. 1:7; 4:12-19

## QUESTIONS FOR CONSIDERATION

1.  At the beginning of this Holy Week, Luke Timothy Johnson bids us consider the "real Jesus" and reconfirm our desire to be radically identified with him. What does Johnson tell us following the "real Jesus" will entail?

_____

_____

_____

_____

_____

_____

_____

2. To speak of the "real Jesus" must mean there is a "false Jesus." What are our temptations to create a "false Jesus"?

_____

_____

_____

_____

_____

_____

_____

_____

3. Throughout Holy Week Jesus will encounter those who seek "to destroy him" (Luke 19:47) because he offered Israel a new and different way of being Israel. It involved a radically different kind of power. What was that different power?

_____

_____

_____

_____

_____

_____

_____

_____

# Tuesday of Holy Week

## MARCH 26, 2024

## READING FOR THE DAY

What love does, it is; what it is, it does—at one and the same moment; simultaneously as it goes beyond itself (in an outward direction) it is in itself (in an inward direction), and simultaneously as it is in itself, it thereby goes beyond itself in such a way that this going beyond and this inward turning, this inward turning and this going beyond, are simultaneously one and the same. . . . Love . . . never thinks about . . . saving oneself, about acquiring confidence itself; the lover in love thinks only about giving confidence and saving another from death. But the lover is not thereby forgotten. . . . God is love, and when a human being, because of love forgets himself, how then should God forget him! No, while the lover forgets himself and thinks of the other person, God thinks of the lover. . . . The lover, who forgets himself, is remembered by love. There is One who thinks of him, and in this way it comes about that the lover gets what he gives.

Søren Kierkegaard, *Works of Love*, trans. Hong, pp. 261-62

## PRAYER

O HOLY LORD, Father Almighty, everlasting God, carry forward in us the gifts of your grace and mercifully bestow upon us by your Spirit what human frailty cannot attain, that we may be both established in perfect faith and conspicuous by the brightness of the joy that comes from the Lord. Preserve in us the inheritance incorruptible, undefiled, and that fades not away. Amen.

Prayers for the Use of the Clergy, in *Ancient Collects and Other Prayers*, p. 179

## FOR REFLECTION

Luke 6:35; John 3:16; 13:34; Rom. 8:35-39; 12:9-21; 13:8-10; 1 Cor. 13:1-13; Eph. 4:1-2; 1 Pet. 4:8-11; 1 John 2:7-11; 3:1-4, 11-18; 4:17-21

## QUESTIONS FOR CONSIDERATION

1. One day during Holy Week Jesus told a parable about some tenants given charge of a vineyard (Luke 20:9-18). In the parable, the tenants loved themselves more than they loved the vineyard owner. Jesus concludes the parable by giving the vineyard to those who love the owner—Jesus— more than they love themselves. Using Kierkegaard, how may you apply Jesus's Holy Week parable to yourself?

_____

_____

_____

_____

_____

_____

_____

_____

_____

2. On another day in Holy Week Jesus saw a poor widow placing two copper coins into the temple treasury (Luke 21:1-4). During this Holy Week, use Kierkegaard and the widow's action to examine your love for Jesus.

_____

_____

_____

_____

_____

_____

_____

_____

3. "What [love] is, it does." How does the meaning of Kierkegaard's statement relate to Philippians 2:5-11?

_____

_____

_____

_____

_____

_____

_____

DAY 37

# Wednesday of Holy Week

MARCH 27, 2024

## READING FOR THE DAY

From the start, Christianity has been rooted in the paradoxical claim that a human being executed as a criminal is the source of God's life-giving and transforming Spirit. From the start, this "good news" has been regarded as foolishness to the wise of the world. Christianity has never been able to "prove" its claims except by appeal to the experiences and convictions of those already convinced. The only real validation for the claim that Christ is what the creed claims . . . , that is, light from light, true God from true God, is to be found in the quality of life demonstrated by those who make this confession.

Only if Christians and Christian communities illustrate lives transformed according to the pattern of faithful obedience and loving service found in Jesus does their claim to live by the Spirit of Jesus have any validity. The claims of the gospel . . . can be validated only . . . by . . . authentic Christian discipleship.

Luke Timothy Johnson, *The Real Jesus*, p. 168

# PRAYER

ALMIGHTY AND EVERLASTING GOD, who enkindles the flame of your love in the hearts of the saints: Grant to us their same faith and power of love, that we may follow their example, letting our "light so shine before men, that they may see [our] good works and [glorify our] Father . . . in heaven." Rejoicing in their witness, may we, too, "bear much fruit," through our Lord and Savior Jesus Christ. Amen.

Adapted from "Saints Days," Prayers for Sacred Seasons, in *Ancient Collects and Other Prayers*, p. 69; Matt. 5:16; John 15:8

## FOR REFLECTION

Isa. 9:6; Matt. 1:18; 5:14-16; Luke 1:26-38; John 1:1-18; 8:48-59; 15:8; Rom. 1:4; 1 Cor. 1:18-30; Phil. 1:27-30; 4:4-9; 1 Tim. 3:16; 1 John 1:1-2; Rev. 1:4-8, 12-16

## QUESTIONS FOR CONSIDERATION

1. "From the start," says Luke Timothy Johnson, the "'good news' has been regarded as foolishness to the wise of the world." Jewish authorities rejected Jesus. In what ways does your culture continue to regard the "good news" as foolishness?

_____

_____

_____

_____

_____

_____

_____

2. Johnson claims that "Christianity has never been able to 'prove' its claims except by appeal to the experiences and convictions of those already convinced." Is he correct? If so, during this Holy Week reflect on how the "convincing" happened to you.

_____

_____

_____

_____

_____

_____

_____


3. Johnson asserts that "only if Christians and Christian communities illustrate lives transformed according to the pattern of faithful obedience and loving service found in Jesus does their claim to live by the Spirit of Jesus have any validity." Reflect on this assertion, and record your thoughts.

_____

_____

_____

_____

_____

_____

_____

_____

# Maundy Thursday

## READING FOR THE DAY

We have learned to believe in the deity of the Son of God from the Son himself. He was betrayed and sold for very little, but he redeems the world at the price of his own blood. As a sheep he is led to the slaughter, but he is Shepherd of Israel, and of the whole world. As a sacrificial lamb he is silent, yet he is the eternal Word of God. He is bruised and wounded, and yet he heals every disease. He is lifted up and nailed to the cross, yet he saved even the robber crucified beside him. On the cross, he wrapped the visible world in darkness. He is given vinegar to drink, but he is altogether the Sweetness that overcomes the bitter taste of sin. He lays down his life but has power to take it again. He rends the veil of the temple and thereby opens for us the doors of heaven. He dies, but he gives life, and by his death he destroys death. He is buried, but he rises again. He goes down into hell, but he releases the captives. He ascends to the Father and will come again to judge the quick and the dead.

What he was (God), he continued to be; what he was not (man), he took to himself.

Gregory of Nazianzus (ca. AD 330-ca. AD 390), "On the Son,"
oration 29, secs. 19-20

## PRAYER

KING OF KINGS, YET BORN OF MARY,
As of old on earth he stood,
Lord of Lords, in human vesture,
In the body and the blood,
He will give to all the faithful
His own self for heavenly food. Amen.

Adapted from The Divine Liturgy of James the Holy Apostle
(ca. AD 150-200), trans. Gerard Moultrie (1864), Hymnary

## FOR REFLECTION

Song of Sol. 5:16; Isa. 53:7, 23; Matt. 6:28; 26:15; 27:51; Luke
23:43; John 1:23; 2:1-11; 10:7-18; 11:43; 19:19; 1 Pet. 1:19

## QUESTIONS FOR CONSIDERATION

1. "Maundy" derives from the Latin word *mandātum,* which
   means "mandate" or "command." On this evening, after
   supper, and after washing the disciples' feet, Jesus said, "A
   new commandment I give to you, that you love one another; even as I have loved you, that you also love one another" (John 13:34). What does it mean to love one another as
   Jesus loved us?

_____

_____

_____

_____

_____

_____

_____

2. In thirteen striking contrasts, Gregory of Nazianzus spells out the meaning of what will happen to Jesus in the coming hours. Take time to reflect on the meaning of each contrast.

_____

_____

_____

_____

_____

_____

3. On this evening, Judas betrayed Jesus. In what ways is Jesus still betrayed today? What are your temptations to betrayal?

_____

_____

_____

_____

_____

_____

4. On this evening, we find Jesus, the eternal Son of God, praying facedown in the garden of Gethsemane (Matt. 26:39). What is happening in this astonishing event?

_____

_____

_____

_____

_____

## READING FOR THE DAY

*First voice.* I stand upon Mount Calvary. My Savior is there, hanging on the cross these three hours, suspended between heaven and earth. The deepest darkness surrounds him. He is absorbed in unutterable grief, feelings of inconceivable anguish, prayers, offerings, and the consummation of our salvation. O my soul, attend this scene and remain in silence, adoration, union. My Jesus, God, Eternity are here, the Blessed Mother Mary, the Beloved Disciple John, holy angels attending!

*Second voice,* from the cross. My Savior, through the darkness, strong, awesome, loud, spoken to the Father in the Highest, resounding to the remote reaches of time and space. "All is consummated!" ALL IS CONSUMMATED! ALL!

*I hear.* My soul plunges still deeper into this abyss of love and the silence of this hour! O think of all that was done for you.

*That voice again!* "Father, into thy hands I commend my spirit." His head sinks down, he breathes his last, nature is convulsed—the horrid crash of rocks and opening tombs resound. JESUS EXPIRES.

Now speak this unspeakable moment in your every breath, in gratitude, love, and silent adoration.

Elizabeth Ann Seton (1774–1821), "The Good Friday . . . ,"
in *Collected Writings: Volume 3b*, pt. 11.21, pp. 37-38

## PRAYER

O LORD JESUS, you have given us everything needed for living a godly life. You have called us to receive your own glory and goodness. By your Spirit cleanse us so that we may wholly love you, be wholly filled with you, and be wholly enlightened and enflamed by you. Amen.

Edward Bouverie Pusey (1800-1882), *Prayers: Ancient and Modern*, p. 267

## FOR REFLECTION

Matt. 27:32-56; Mark 15:16-47; Luke 23:26-56; John 19:1-27; 1 Cor. 1:18-25; Eph. 2:14-22; Col. 1:20; Heb. 12:2

## QUESTIONS FOR CONSIDERATION

1. With Elizabeth Ann Seton, pray, "O my soul, attend this scene and remain in silence, adoration, union."

_____

_____

_____

_____

_____

_____

_____

_____

2. The Gospel of Matthew names Jesus "Emman'u-el . . . God with us" (Matt. 1:23). Contemplate the content of Jesus's name and identity as you wait before the cross.

_____

_____

_____

_____

_____

3. Luke tells us that in the temple, when Jesus was an infant, Simeon told Mary, "A sword will pierce through your own soul also" (Luke 2:35). Contemplate the "sword" piercing Mary's heart on this day as she waits before the cross.

_____

_____

_____

_____

_____

4. On this day, Paul tells us, Christ triumphed over all the powers that stand against us and God's creation (Col. 2:13-15). Contemplate the powers over which Christ triumphed.

_____

_____

_____

_____

_____

_____

# Holy Saturday

## MARCH 30, 2024

## READING FOR THE DAY

Apart from Christ's resurrection, apart from the reappearance of the historical Christ as the personal ground and cause of the disciples' faith, there is no conceivable basis for explaining what happened after the crucifixion. In one bold stroke the death of Christ had annihilated everything Jesus's disciples had hoped for about his being the Messiah. Their defeat was conclusive. If everything they had hoped for had been finally destroyed by Jesus's death, and nothing more ever heard from them, the outcome would have been understandable. True, it is abstractly possible that after the first blow of Christ's death, the deep spiritual impressions Christ had made upon the disciples might have in some way revived and operated upon them in some powerful way. But to understand what the apostles did afterward, to explain their transition from absolute dejection to the expansive and powerful rebirth of their faith, something must have happened in the chain of events that only Christ's resurrection can explain. Their wrecked confidence in Jesus's promises was restored only because Christ himself, raised from the dead, repeated his promises to them. That was the rebirth of a communion with Christ never to be dissolved, but ever growing more and more.

Augustus Neander (1789–1850), *The Life of Jesus Christ*,
bk. V, pt. II, chap. VIII, sec. 295

## PRAYER

O GOD, who hast promised that you will always be present
with your church to the end of the age and that the gates
of hell shall never prevail against the apostolic confession,
graciously make your strength perfect in our weakness and
show the efficacy of your promises by dwelling in even the
most feeble saints. Amen.

*"For the Church," Intercessions, in*
*Ancient Collects and Other Prayers, pp. 97-98*

## FOR REFLECTION

Matt. 26:69-75; 28:1-10, 16-20; Mark 14:43-50, 66-72; 16:1-8;
Luke 23:26-31; 24:13-24; John 20:19-23; 1 Cor. 15:12-19

## QUESTIONS FOR CONSIDERATION

1. On this day—Holy Saturday, Easter Eve—our crucified
   Lord lay dead in the tomb. On this day, Christ's church
   considers the world of darkness that would exist without
   the resurrection. Reflect on that darkness, a darkness in
   which many still live.

_____

_____

_____

_____

_____

_____

_____

2. Reflect on the absolute horror and disenchantment experienced by Jesus's disciples on this day so long ago. Put yourself in their place. Would you have responded differently?

_____

_____

_____

_____

_____

_____

_____

_____

_____

3. On this special day, Christ's church waits and reviews the season of Lent. Are there areas of self-examination you have yet to make as you await the Easter celebration?

_____

_____

_____

_____

_____

_____

_____

_____

_____

_____

# Easter Sunday

## MARCH 31, 2024

## READING FOR THE DAY

On this day Christ rose from the dead. May he today renew me by the Holy Spirit, clothe me with the new humanity, and bestow upon me his new creation.

On Good Friday the Lamb was slain and the doorposts were anointed. Egypt bewailed her firstborn, the destroyer passed over us, the seal of blood was dreadful and revered, and we were walled in by the precious blood. Today, Easter, we have escaped Egypt and from Pharaoh. Now, no one can restrain us from celebrating a feast to the Lord our God—the feast of our departure. We feast, not with the old leaven of malice and wickedness, but with the unleavened bread of sincerity and truth. We carry with us nothing of the old Egyptian leaven.

On Good Friday I was crucified with Christ; today I am glorified with him. Yesterday I died with Christ; today I rise with him. Yesterday I was buried with my Lord; today from the tomb I rise with him.

Let us offer to him ourselves, the possession most precious to God. In the triumphant Christ let us recognize our dignity, let us honor our Archetype, and let us know the power of the mystery and why Christ died.

Gregory of Nazianzus, "On Easter and His Reluctance
[to accept ordination to the priesthood]," oration 1, secs. 2-4

## PRAYER

O CHRIST, bring again our daylight; day returns with you!
Hell today is vanquished; heaven is won today! Amen.

Venantius Honorius Clementianus Fortunatus (ca. AD 530–609),
trans. John Ellerton (1868), Hymnary

## FOR REFLECTION

Exod. 12:1–30; Isa. 65:5; Matt. 28:1–10; Mark 16:1–13; Luke
24:1–12; John 1:35–36; 20:1–18; Acts 2:14–36; 1 Cor. 5:8; Rev.
5:6–14

## QUESTIONS FOR CONSIDERATION

1. The entire Christian faith rises or falls on the resurrection of Jesus Christ by the power of the Holy Spirit. Most fundamentally, how do we know the Father raised his Son from the grave?

_____

_____

_____

_____

_____

2. Gregory of Nazianzus celebrates: "Today, Easter, we have escaped Egypt and from Pharaoh." What does he mean?

_____

_____

_____

_____

3. The apostle Paul tells us that apart from Easter our faith is in vain (1 Cor. 15:12–18). But because of Easter we live in anticipation of our own resurrection. Contemplate the hope of the resurrection as it relates to your life and death?

_____

_____

_____

_____

_____

_____

_____

4. Ask the Holy Spirit to blend your Easter celebration with the suffering church on this day of Jesus's resurrection, and pray for Christ's church wherever it celebrates today.

_____

_____

_____

_____

_____

_____

_____

## "Hallelujah! Christ is risen! The Lord is risen indeed."

# Notes

1. "The Glory of These Forty Days," attributed to Gregory the Great (540–604), trans. Maurice F. Bell (1862–1947).

2. Claudia Frances Hernaman (1838-98), "Lord, Who throughout These Forty Days" (1873).

3. Brian Kolodiejchuk notes that it is difficult to understand what "darkness" meant for Mother Teresa at this time. Eventually the term would characterize interior suffering and a deficit of divine consolation. She would know periods of spiritual leanness and an absence of the sense of God's presence. But never was there any dearth in her longing for God. Brian Kolodiejchuk, ed., *Mother Teresa: Come Be My Light; The Private Writings of the "Saint of Calcutta"* (New York: Doubleday, 2007), 21-22.

4. John H. Walton, *Ancient Near Eastern Thought and the Old Testament* (Grand Rapids: Baker Academic, 2006), 212.

# Sources

American Catholic Sermons. Special Collections. Georgetown University Library.

Anselm. *St. Anselm's Book of Meditations and Prayers.* London: Burns and Gates, 1872. Reprint, Christian Classics Ethereal Library. http://www.ccel.org/ccel/anselm/meditations.html.

*Ante-Nicene Fathers.* 10 vols. Reprint of the 1885 edition, Christian Classics Ethereal Library. http://www.ccel.org/fathers.html.

*Apostolic Fathers.* Translated by J. B. Lightfoot. Edited and completed by J. R. Harmer. 1891. Reprint of 1956 Baker Book House edition, Christian Classics Ethereal Library. http://www.ccel.org/ccel/lightfoot/fathers.titlepage.html.

Arndt, Johann. *True Christianity: A Treatise on Sincere Repentance, True Faith, the Holy Walk of the True Christian, Etc.* Philadelphia: Lutheran Book Store, 1868. Reprint, Project Gutenberg, 2010. http://www.gutenberg.org/files/34736/34736-h/34736-h.html #toc355.

Bonhoeffer, Dietrich. *The Cost of Discipleship.* 2nd ed. London: SCM Press, 1959. Reprint, New York: Macmillan, 1963.

Book of Common Prayer. New York: Church Hymnal Corporation, 1979. http://justus.anglican.org/resources/bcp/formatted_1979.htm.

Bright, William. *Ancient Collects and Other Prayers, Selected for Devotional Use from Various Rituals.* Oxford, UK: J. H. and Jas. Parker, 1864. Internet Archive. https://archive.org/details/ancient collects00collgoog/page/n3/mode/1up?view=theater.

Brueggemann, Walter. *The Bible Makes Sense.* Louisville, KY: Westminster John Knox Press, 2001.

Bunsen, Baron. *Prayers from the Collection of the Late Baron Bunsen.* Translated by Catherine Winkworth. London: Longmans, Green, 1871. Internet Archive. https://archive.org/stream/prayers 00bunsgoog#page/n176/mode/2up.

Calvin, John. *Institutes of the Christian Religion.* Translated by
Henry Beveridge. Edinburgh: Calvin Translation Society, 1845.
Reprint, CCEL. http://www.ccel.org/ccel/calvin/institutes.

Catherine of Genoa. *The Life and Doctrine of Saint Catherine of Genoa.* New York: Christian Press Association, 1907. Reprint, CCEL.
http://www.ccel.org/ccel/catherine_g/life.txt.

Catherine of Siena. *The Letters of Catherine Benincasa.* Translated
by Vida D. Scudder. Reprint of the 1905 edition, Project Gutenberg,
2005. http://www.gutenberg.org/cache/epub/7403/pg7403.html.

Chrysostom, John. *The Divine Liturgy of St. John Chrysostom.* Or-
thodox.net. http://www.orthodox.net/services/sluzebnic
-chrysostom.pdf.

*A Collection of Hymns for the Use of the People Called Methodists.*
1889. http://www.ccel.org/w/wesley/hymn/jw.html#index.

Cranmer, Thomas. *The Works of Thomas Cranmer, Archbishop of
Canterbury, Martyr, 1556.* Edited by John Edmund Cox. Vol. 2.
Cambridge: University Press, 1846. Google Books. http://books
.google.com/books?id=DQw5AQAAMAAJ&printsec=frontcover
&dq=Thomas+Cranmer & hl=en&sa=X&ei=L3FpUq2jOdWo 4AO
tiYGIBA&ved=0 CE 8Q6AEwBg#v=onepage&q=Thomas%20Cran
mer&f=false.

Donne, John. *John Donne's Devotions.* 1624. Reprint, Christian Classics Ethereal Library. http://www.ccel.org/ccel/donne/devotions.

Forsyth, Peter T. *The Work of Christ.* London: Hodder and Stoughton,
1910. Reprint, CCEL. http://www.ccel.org/ccel/forsyth/work.txt.

Graham, Billy. *The Holy Spirit: Activating God's Power in Your Life.*
Waco, TX: Word Books, 1978. Reprint, Nashville: Thomas Nelson,
2000.

Hymnary.org. http://www.hymnary.org/texts?qu=+in:texts.

Johnson, Luke Timothy. *The Real Jesus: The Misguided Quest for
the Historical Jesus and the Truth of the Traditional Gospels.* New
York: HarperSanFrancisco, 1996.

Kierkegaard, Søren. *Edifying Discourses: A Selection.* Edited by
Paul L. Holmer. Translated by David F. Swenson and Lillian M.
Swenson. New York: Harper and Brothers, 1958. Internet Archive.
https://archive.org/details/edify ingdiscours00kier.

————. *Eighteen Upbuilding Discourses.* Edited and translated by Howard V. Hong and Edna H. Hong. Princeton, NJ: Princeton University Press, 1990.

————. *Selections from the Writings of Kierkegaard* (cited as *Selections* in text). Translated by L. M. Hollander. University of Texas Bulletin 2326. Austin, TX: University of Texas, 1923. Internet Archive. https://archive.org/stream/selectionsfromwr00kieruoft #page/n1/mode/2up.

————. *Works of Love.* Translated by Howard and Edna Hong. New York: Harper and Brothers, 1962.

Limehouse, Frank F., III. Prayers contributed to *The Book of Saints: The Modern Era.* Edited by Al Truesdale. Kansas City: Beacon Hill Press of Kansas City, 2018.

Luther, Martin. *On the Freedom of a Christian* (or *A Treatise on Christian Liberty*). 1520. In vol. 2, *Works of Martin Luther, with Introductions and Notes.* Translated by J. J. Schindel and C. M. Jacobs. Philadelphia: A. J. Holman Co., 1915. Reprint, Project Gutenberg, 2011. http://www.gutenberg.org/files/34904/34904-0.txt.

Macarius-Symeon. *Fifty Spiritual Homilies of St. Macarius the Egyptian.* Translated by A. J. Mason. London: Society for Promoting Christian Knowledge, 1921. http://archive.org/stream/fifty spiritualho00pseuuoft/fiftyspiritualho 00pseuuoft_djvu.txt.

Mother Teresa. *Mother Teresa: Come Be My Light; The Private Writings of the "Saint of Calcutta."* Edited by Brian Kolodiejchuk. New York: Doubleday, 2007.

Neander, Augustus. *The Life of Jesus Christ in Its Historical Connexion and Historical Development.* New York: Harper and Brothers, 1870. Reprint, CCEL. http://www.ccel.org/ccel/neander_a/life.txt.

Newman, John Henry. *Parochial and Plain Sermons.* Vol. 7. London: Longmans, Green, 1891. Reprint, Project Gutenberg, 2008. http:// www.gutenberg.org/cache/epub/24256/pg24256.txt.

*Nicene and Post-Nicene Fathers*, Series I (14 vols.), Series II (14 vols.). Edited by Philip Schaff. Reprint of the 1885 edition. Christian Classics Ethereal Library. http://www.ccel.org/fathers.html.

Nouwen, Henri J. M. *The Way of the Heart: Connecting with God through Prayer, Wisdom, and Silence.* Minneapolis: Seabury Press, 1981.

*Services for Congregational Worship.* Rev. ed. Boston: American Unitarian Association, 1877. Internet Archive. https://archive.org/stream/servcongr 00amer#page/n7/mode/2up.

Seton, Elizabeth Ann. *Collected Writings: Volume 3b* (2006). Vincentian Digital Books. Book 10. http://via.library.depaul.edu/vincen tian_ebooks/10.

*Sing to the Lord.* Kansas City: Lillenas Publishing Company, 1993.

Smith, Hannah Whitall. *The God of All Comfort.* 1870. Reprint, CCEL. http://www.ccel.org/ccel/smith_hw/comfort.i.html.

ten Boom, Corrie. *Corrie ten Boom's Prison Letters.* Fort Washington, PA: CLC Publications, 2015.

Teresa of Ávila. *The Way of Perfection.* 1566. London: Sheed and Ward, 1946. Reprint of 1964 New York: Image Books/Doubleday edition, CCEL. http://www.ccel.org/ccel/teresa/way.txt.

Tileston, Mary Wilder. *Prayers: Ancient and Modern.* New York: Doubleday and McClure, 1897. Internet Archive. https://archive.org/details/prayersancienta00tilegoog.

Wesley, John. *A Plain Account of Christian Perfection.* Wesley Center Online. http://wesley.nnu.edu/john-wesley/a-plain-account-of-christian-perfection/.

Wheatley, Richard. *The Life and Letters of Mrs. Phoebe Palmer.* New York: W. C. Palmer, 1881. Internet Archive. https://archive.org/stream/lifelettersofmr00whea#page/n7/mode/2up.

Whitefield, George. *Selected Sermons of George Whitefield* (cited as *Selected Sermons* in text). N.d. Reprint, CCEL. http://www.ccel.org/ccel/whitefield/sermons.txt. (See Thomas S. Kidd, *George Whitefield: America's Spiritual Founding Father* [New Haven, CT: Yale University Press, 2014].)

Wilberforce, William. *A Practical View of the Prevailing Religious System of Professed Christians, in the Higher and Middle Classes in This Country, Contrasted with Real Christianity.* Dublin: Robert Dapper, 1797. Reprint, Project Gutenberg, 2008. http://www.gutenberg.org/cache/epub/25709/pg25709.txt.utf8.

Wright, N. T. *For All God's Worth: True Worship and the Calling of the Church.* Grand Rapids: Eerdmans, 1997.